Tending the Soul
With
Healing Ritual

Gay Wolff, Ph.D.

All rights reserved. No part of this book shall be reproduced or transmitted in any form or by any means, electronic, mechanical, magnetic, photographic including photocopying, recording or by any information storage and retrieval system, without prior written permission of the publisher. No patent liability is assumed with respect to the use of the information contained herein. Although every precaution has been taken in the preparation of this book, the publisher and author assume no responsibility for errors or omissions. Neither is any liability assumed for damages resulting from the use of the information contained herein.

Copyright © 2016 by Gay Wolff, Ph.D.

ISBN 978-1-4958-0948-4
Library of Congress Control Number: 2016901638

Proofreading services provided by Shannon Sloan-Spice, Ph.D.
Interior layout design services provided by Dana White, Ph.D.

Published March 2016

INFINITY PUBLISHING
1094 New DeHaven Street, Suite 100
West Conshohocken, PA 19428-2713
Toll-free (877) BUY BOOK
Local Phone (610) 941-9999
Fax (610) 941-9959
Info@buybooksontheweb.com
www.buybooksontheweb.com

Dedication

Many people have assisted my personal soul-tending process over the years, and it is to them I want to dedicate this book. First and foremost, I must thank and honor my husband, Kurtis Wolff, who has always supported my seeking, teaching, and writing ventures.

I also honor the many teachers and mentors, as well as clients and students, who have fostered my soul journey through the decades and helped me to discover the healing power of Ritual.

Finally, I wish to further dedicate this book to you, the reader. May the ideas and Rituals offered here assist your own soul-tending journey.

~gw

Tending the Soul With Healing Ritual

Table of Contents

Part 1: The Healing Power of Ritual..1

Chapter 1: Understanding Ritual.................................5
   Why Ritual?..7
   The Mythic Nature of Ritual..10
   Beyond Art & Psychology..13
   Stepping into Ritual..15
   Living Energy..17
   Sensing Subtle Energy..22

Chapter 2: Creating Ritual..27
   Spiritual Ceremony versus Ritual...................................28
   Opening the Axis Mundi...29
   Five Components of Ritual..31
      Working in Ayni...31
      Reverent Intent..33
      Sacred Space - Invoking the Numinous...................35
      Ritual Drama - Engaging the Numinous.................41
      Closing Space..44

Part 2: Rituals Menu & Guide 47

Chapter 3: Earth 49
   Sandpaintings: Mandala Rituals 51
      Sandpainting 1: Clearing and Releasing 53
      Sandpainting 2: Mythic Mirror 56
   Darkspring Khuya Ritual: The Clearing Stone 61
   Harmony Ritual: Attune With Nature 67

Chapter 4: Water 73
   Rainbow Shower 76
   Florida Water 78
   Reflection Pool Ritual 86

Chapter 5: Air 91
   Sun & Moon Salutation 92
   Walking Mantra Meditation 96

Chapter 6: Fire 109
   Fire Ceremony 110
   Fire Breaking Ice Ritual 116

Chapter 7: Conclusion 123
Rituals List Appendix 127
Resources Appendix & Cited Sources 129
Index 133
About the Author 135

The primary difference between the western and indigenous ways of life is that Indians experience and relate to a living universe, whereas western people reduce all things, living or not, to objects.

~ Vine Deloria, Jr. (In Interview with Derek Jensen)

Tending the Soul With Healing Ritual

Part 1
The Healing Power of Ritual

A ritual is the enactment of a myth. By participating in the ritual, you are participating in the myth. And since myth is a projection of the depth wisdom of the psyche, by participating in a ritual,... you are being, as it were, put in accord with that wisdom, which is the wisdom that is inherent within you anyhow. Your consciousness is being reminded of the wisdom of your own life.
~ Joseph Campbell ("The Wisdom of J.C." Interviews)

People need Rituals. In today's modern Western culture of progress and perpetual striving, the reflective qualities of religion, meditation, and ritual reside in the margins of our daily living. Yet many Western psyches yearn for a deeper experience with life and its mysteries. Despite the dominance of a material and scientific world-view, on a personal level, people still crave something more beautiful and meaningful than what materiality and the analytics of logic can offer.

All of us yearn for meaning in life. We want to be moved, to feel loved, valued, and connected. Everywhere we turn, we feel the pressures of the material and rational world-views. Many of us are drawn into the belief that having more of something—knowledge, stuff, time, position—will improve the character of our existence, or make us happy.

Even as we rush to meet deadlines and objectives, we yearn for fulfillment—for something more than what the common life offers. We know material things won't sustain or nourish us. But, what will? To find the something more that nourishes our souls, we must go deeper than the common realms of mainstream reality.

Mainstream existence is defined by the workings of the conscious mind. Yet, our conscious minds reflect only a fraction of who we are, how we really think, and how we relate to the universe. And this is where the importance of Ritual is demonstrated. Rituals offer ways to go beyond the restrictions of the conscious mind so as to nourish and balance the whole human—our body, our psyche, our soul and our relationships. Incorporating Ritual in our lifestyles provides a metaphysical foundation by which we can sustain and nourish ourselves and our loved ones.

In Part One of this book, I explain why people still need Rituals today and how enacting Ritual can help us to awaken and heal our deepest Self.

Part Two provides a menu and guide for personal Rituals designed to stimulate healing and transformational shifts. Most of these Rites are drawn from my accumulated work or re-inventions of mythic concepts. However, some of these are my adaptations of core processes I learned from others whom I wish to acknowledge. The Sandpainting and Fire Ceremony Rites are adaptations from Alberto Villoldo's teachings, the unwinding *chakras* portion of the Rainbow Shower I first learned from

Deepak Chopra, and the Sun and Moon salutations are adaptations of yoga. It is my hope that as you journey through these pages, you will find yourself walking a path of self-discovery and inner beauty.

Tending the Soul With Healing Ritual

1: Understanding Ritual

*I believe that if your culture or tradition doesn't have
the specific ritual you are craving, then you are
absolutely permitted to make up a ceremony of your own
devising, fixing your own broken-down emotional systems with
all the do-it-yourself resourcefulness of a generous plumber/poet.*
~ Elizabeth Gilbert (Eat, Pray, Love)

Beyond the occasional cultural ceremonies we think of as rituals, such as weddings or graduations, we need embodied moments that allow us to open the windows of our inner being to let our soul expand, ventilate, and be refreshed. These moments connect us to the world beyond us and reinforce our place within it.

The kind of spiritual or mythic Ritual I am describing here is distinguished with a capital R. Through such a mythic Ritual process, the body, mind, and heart can be brought into alignment, which allows us to achieve harmony with the living and divine world. Through Ritual we can bypass the conscious, rational mind and utilize our intuitive sensibilities to access our heart's wisdom. From this state of reverence and receptivity, we can reclaim a personal and direct relationship with the power of creation, and join many others in becoming co-creators of reality.

Throughout this text, I use the terms "the Sacred" and "the Divine" interchangeably to refer to the various transpersonal forces that exist naturally in the multi-dimensional universe. These include spirit guides, aspects of nature, and psychological forces that are part of the mythic cosmos. To be more specific, beyond the Creator or Great Spirit, the Sacred includes manifestations of divinity that infuse creation with that mysterious essence that intuitive people often sense below and above everyday existence. In religious terms, the Sacred begins with the Creator and includes, other gods, angels, guides, power places and entities, and living energies such as the Holy Spirit and *qi*. Psychologically, the Sacred includes the full range of archetypal forces, our unconscious or higher Self, and the collective or transpersonal unconscious.

For millennia, Rituals have served seekers, sages, mystics, and shamans in cultivating a relationship with these divine forces. Through the intuitive capacities of Ritual, these sages have engaged both internal and transpersonal subtle realities. The techniques of Ritual create access and opportunities for wisdom and healing, but whether we can learn from Ritual depends upon our ability to open and to trust. Sacred Rituals function independently of, but in harmony with, cultural and religious beliefs and can be adapted to virtually anyone's religious, spiritual, or psychological disposition.

1: Understanding Ritual

Why Ritual?

The purpose of Ritual is to bring us closer to the source of our being, where we can clear patterns and shift things more easily in order to understand and change the material reality. Imagine standing by a river where suddenly all your personal possessions are washing down its swift current. Like most of us, you might try to rescue your possessions one soggy piece at a time. Yet, I suspect that many of us would also eventually venture upstream to discover who is throwing our things into the water.

Similarly, we can opt to merely treat symptoms on the surface level and accept the temporary relief of surface remedies. However, to actually heal our physical and psychological ailments, we must seek out their sources. For, when we access our being at the subtle energy level, when we identify the root causes of our afflictions, we can make "upstream" changes to improve our lives on multiple planes, including the emotional and physical.

Ritual is not about having power *over* the Sacred. Rather, it is about being empowered *through* or *with* the Sacred, and activating our own divine nature. With an attitude of reciprocation and balance (what Peruvian shamans call *ayni*), we can access our spiritual power, and the divine forces that inform, enrich, and heal our lives.

Performing Ritual involves our participation in several aspects. At the most physical level, the body is engaged in a ceremonial act. The heart-wisdom is accessed to determine your intent. The imagination (intuition) directs the flow of the Rite, and emotions drive the desire that motivates it. Beyond the body, mind, and emotions of the process, Ritual also works energetically to clear, repair, and make shifts in our *luminous* field. This energy body—also called our subtle, light, or luminous body—is part of the material world, but at a fundamental and subtle level.

The Eastern concepts of an auric field and the *chakras* are widely known today throughout the West, and in the past century, they have become influential. However, many people do not realize that the concept of a light body, including meridians and the centers of light, have also long been recognized throughout shamanic and mystical traditions across the globe.

Perennial mysticism has taught us that Ritual is one of the most direct means of gaining access to the flow of creative energy that is universally understood to be essential to life. We know this living energy by many names: *Qi, Chi, Ki, Tao, Reiki, Prana, Mana,* the *Holy Spirit,* and in Peruvian shamanism, *kawsay.* Soul and spirit are much more subtle than the light body, but by working at the light body level, we are working further upstream—reaching beyond the limits and patterns of our physical body, mind, and energetic resources—toward the levels of Soul and Spirit.

In mysticism, access to both personal and transpersonal mystical domains is understood to happen through a central channel known as the *axis mundi*, the axis of the world. This channel is depicted mythically in a variety of forms, including a sacred tree, a central corridor, a pillar, a ladder, or a hole in the roof. Yet, it is always understood to exist within ourselves, and thus the way to access this path is through the deep interiors of the psyche, which we engage with our intuitive and imaginal faculties. The imagination, therefore, is a gateway into the subtle domains—those transpersonal realms of the living cosmos and those areas within ourselves

1: Understanding Ritual

that are imbued with the Soul that is uniquely ours. Ritual offers many mystical opportunities, but for our purposes here, we will focus on the personal potentials of Ritual, in particular, the psychological and energetic healing benefits.

The Rituals in this book will guide your soul work to help you engage at an energetic level, where you can access the power to change and heal. Personal Rites can help you to clarify uncertainties and to shift imprints or patterns that are restricting or distorting aspects of your life. This will enable you to reclaim your personal and direct relationship with the divine powers of creation so that you can awaken your innate ability to be a co-creator of your own life and our shared world.

In our modern culture of busy-ness in work and play, many of us have lost touch with how to spiritually engage and recharge ourselves. Since you are reading this book, it is likely that you, like me, have felt something missing from the life you are living—you may feel emptiness where there should be substance. Even if you seem to have a good life, you may feel that your existence, in part or whole, is lacking in meaning or soulful depths.

Psychologically, you may feel at the mercy of the plots and characters that make up the drama of your life. Even if you have a religious or meditative practice that provides some means for managing these influences, you may find that you still desire a better understanding, greater influence, or a deeper experience with that *something more* that is resonating in your heart.

Ritual offers a means to open a dialogue and to regain a personal relationship with both the interior and transpersonal Sacred. It provides a way to harmonize your body, mind, and soul (as well as your relationships with others) for a feeling of congruence, meaningfulness, and ultimately, a deeper joy in living.

You can bring Ritual into your individual and family customs without changing the dynamic of the life you enjoy with family and friends. By this, I mean that Ritual is a personal act that can be adapted and tailored to your family's personality and setting, as long as the basic elements of Ritual are in place.

The Mythic Nature of Ritual

Though we hear the term Ritual used frequently to refer to routines or special customs that we embrace, such as New Year's or Thanksgiving, the kind of Ritual we are speaking of here is something deeper—more spiritual, more personal, and simultaneously, more transpersonal or *mythic*. Today, the word "myth" is taken to mean something that is commonly believed even though it is a fiction or something unknown. However, before the philosophical rise of rationalism in the 17th century, the myths of the world had always been understood to be the most true and most sacred stories and wisdom teachings of a culture.

The fathers of rationalism, Descartes and Newton, certainly believed in God, and they were deeply motivated to determine the true nature of existence. However well intentioned, their theories birthed philosophies of disbelief rather than belief, which gave rise to world-views that are both agnostic and skeptical. The great gift of the agnosticism of science and rationalism is that it liberated us to seek truth independently, leading to philosophical and religious freedoms never before known.

1: Understanding Ritual

However, in the 20th century, quantum physics and other scientific approaches validated many of the truths known to us through myths. For example, archeo-astronomy has demonstrated that some myths are accurate symbolic accounts of cosmic happenings. Other studies have verified that just as planets are named as gods in myths, their energetic personalities are observably reflected in human patterns. Especially relevant to our topic, quantum physics has shown that consciousness influences matter and all matter is interconnected and interrelated. This validates key elements of the mystical belief that we live in a conscious and holistic cosmos and that intention can influence reality. [1]

While myth is a known vehicle for deep truths, it is not necessarily factual. Like poetry, myths are symbolic and archetypal in nature, which means they resonate with meaning on multiple levels, and only sometimes or only in part reflect a purely material fact. When Robert Frost wrote, "Poetry begins with a lump in the throat," he captured a truth without being biologically factual. His symbolic sentence resonates expansive qualities at the heart of poetry that a scientific explanation might never capture.

The fathers of depth psychology, Sigmund Freud and Carl Jung, recognized that myth arises not from the conscious and calculating mind, but rather from the unconscious mind wherein we are connected to deeper truths: inner landscapes long explored by mystics, shamans, healers, and soul-journeyers like you and me. Myths come from those shadowy

---

[1] For further research on these comments, you might begin your reading with Richard Tarnas's *Psyche and Cosmos* and Bohm & Hiley's book *The Undivided Universe*.

domains where dreams and intuition function, and they arise to inspire, educate, and guide us when needed.

At some point, we have all recognized an essence of truth that we knew with our heart or our gut but that may have differed from what reason told us. We now know that our stomachs actually have brain cells, and that our hearts send more information to the brain than the other way around.[2] We are just beginning to understand the deep intelligence of the heart and the body. Despite what is often suggested, we are not purely or even mostly logical *thinkers*. Rather, we are more naturally psychosomatic thinkers and intuitive *knowers*. It is no accident that artists often provide us with powerful insights or creative expressions that move us deeply. Great artists create from their inner depths: that mythic Self that harbors one's deepest beliefs and driving passions. Some artists even unveil archetypal truths that inspire us and resonate at levels so deep that we may never understand why or how they move us.

I use the term *mythic* to invoke the deep spiritual and authentic realm that we access through the imaginal mind—the intuitive mind. This is the realm of myth and archetypes. It lies beyond concrete or measurable knowing, beyond the mind's rational processes. It includes our psychological depths, the innate wisdom of our body (somatic wisdom), our subtle energy realms, the mystical legacy of the ages, and the multitudes of archetypal and transpersonal forces described by myths, mystics, and poets.

---

[2] See more at heartmath.org.

1: Understanding Ritual

There has been a great deal of interest in the power of intention in recent decades, yet how *does* one channel one's intention? How do we quiet the chatter of the perceiving, remembering mind? How do we find our inner *axis mundi*? Most of us find it difficult to settle our thoughts and keep our minds quiet for more than a few seconds at the time during meditation, despite dedicated practices. Yet, throughout the ages, there have been mystics who have achieved great intuitive power. Instead of waiting passively for intuitive insight to become revealed, we can learn to engage the healing depths of our own psyche, and perhaps the Divine Other. Through Ritual, words, images, sounds, and actions provide ways for us to focus and channel our thoughts, and therefore direct our energy. At this mythic level, we can engage the soul, the Self, and the planes of archetypal forces that will help us to develop, shift, release, or heal, and sometimes access wisdom from beyond. However, unlike science, mythic knowledge comes with believing first—or at least, letting go of disbelief enough to be receptive to what *could* happen—and what *might* happen. If the rational mind's mantra is "seeing is believing," the intuitive mind's mantra is "believing is seeing."

Beyond Art & Psychology

Depth Psychology suggests that the intuitive imagination, like that at the source of myth and art, reflects hidden aspects of who we are, who we are becoming, and what we need or fear at an unconscious level. Therapeutically utilizing free-flow art and Jung's Active Imagination techniques can provide wonderfully healing results. Because they are primarily tools of open expression, they tend to generate spontaneous and often surprising, though authentic revelations.

In contrast, Ritual directs and thus creates a focus for the imagination by guiding one through specific physical and intuitive processes, yielding results that, although also unpredictable, are usually relevant to the intent of the Ritual. Both processes have their value: the uninhibited releasing of the unconscious through art and Active Imagination techniques and, in contrast, the directed intent of imaginal intelligence through the guided visualization of Ritual. In this resource, Ritual is used as a means of bringing personal empowerment into your life at the emotional, psychological, energetic, and spiritual levels. It is offered as a resource for making changes where conscious techniques have failed to provide the results you seek.

Through Ritual, we bypass our conscious, rational minds to access the intuitive heart and the *intelligence* of the soul, which also shifts our energetic patterns. The body, mind, and heart are brought into alignment, which allows us to gain insight from and create influence upon the subtle dimensions of reality where we access intuitive wisdom. You may think of these domains in psychological terms as your higher Self or what Jung named the Collective Unconscious. You may prefer David Bohm's quantum theory of the super-implicate order. You might also accept these states as metaphysical domains described by perennial mysticism. Regardless of how you choose to frame these subtle realms, *Ritual takes us closer to the blueprint of our being where we can clear and shift things more easily, and ultimately change our reality.*

1: Understanding Ritual

Modern research, on many fronts including quantum physics, has shown that consciousness *does* actually exert influence upon the material world. Thus, when we prepare for and perform a Ritual, we are engaging the conscious living energy of the cosmos directly, personally, and intimately. We become co-creative partners with the Sacred because Ritual takes us beyond the psychological. It does more than calm the mind and heart. It is a process of thinning the veils between the dimensions of the material world and those luminous realms lying within and beyond oneself. *In Ritual, the ordinary becomes extraordinary, certainty becomes mystery, and potentialities become real possibilities!*

Stepping into Ritual

Ritual is an embodied imaginal experience, requiring both our body and imagination to be engaged. Therefore, it is not enough to simply go through the motions, parroting a technique. One must enter into the Ritual drama as a player. In earnest Ritual, we let the world and its judgments slip into the periphery of our vision. We place ourselves inside the *sacred story*—the mythic core that gives structure and meaning to our Ritual. As our conscious perceptions and judgments dim, we begin to feel ourselves come into alignment with the living Universe, the Divine, or our truest selves. Thus every Ritual has both personal and archetypal qualities that weave its mythic nature. The limits and possibilities of a Rite depend on your level of engagement.

The question arises, then, as to what specifically distinguishes a mythically meaningful *Ritual* (with a capital R) from an ordinary or common *ritual*? The mythic Ritual process I describe here depends upon three key steps: a mindful and deliberate act, the embodiment of a mythic concept or purpose, and an intention to transform or transcend that which is ordinary or conscious.

Ritual is not done so much to celebrate or expedite ordinary events, but rather to facilitate an exceptional experience outside the ordinary patterns of life. This contrast is so essential that Ritual begins with the act of a separation from the *profane* (ordinary, everyday) world—distinguishing between the two interlinked domains of existence—the *sacred* and *profane*—what Mircea Eliade calls the "two modes of being in the world" (*The Sacred and Profane* 14).

Since Rituals include many characteristics that overlap with those of ordinary life (such as location, art, dancing, eating, washing, and singing), great care is given to the beginnings of the Ritual process by means of establishing an exalted space-time setting that I refer to as *Sacred Space*. This is a fluid, transitory time and place that is separate from the everyday world in which daily life takes place.

Native Americans often perform Rituals in houses or huts that are seemingly ordinary until their use in Ritual transforms them into sacred places. In his book *Yuwipi*, William Powers points out that the Oglala sweat lodge frame, when not in use, is ordinarily so disregarded that dogs walk through, sometimes relieving themselves on it. However, when the time comes to use it for a Rite, a process of reverent preparation transforms the ordinary place into Sacred Space, where people can engage Spirit.

While the physical space and act of Ritual are indeed significant, the *attitude* of being completely present and mythically engaged during the

1: Understanding Ritual

Ritual is what makes a Rite a creative experience—thus activating the transformative powers of Creation.

In simple terms, *Ritual is a personal act with transpersonal intent*. This means that we use our body in a way that is infused with an intention to reach beyond the mundane linear space-time of the material world. We seek guidance, connection, healing, power or inspiration from a source deeper or higher than that of our conscious minds. We can be co-creators of our lives and our reality in order to heal, achieve desires, and evolve for the better. I invite you to join me in a journey to re-infuse your life with spiritual meaning and connection, and harmonize the soul with the Sacred.

Living Energy

Shamanism, a pragmatic mysticism that is the oldest and most universally adapted form of religion, is a practice of direct mystical experience with the Sacred. Ancient cultures relied on the heavenly bodies, nature, and their intuitive abilities to guide them in their struggle to thrive. Shamans could heal the ills of their people or gain divine insights, such as where game would be for the hunt or when their tribe should migrate. The cycles of life were observed not only in the seasons, but also in the patterns of the cosmos. The religions of the ages have similar mystical roots, as is reflected in the mythic record, found in archeology, artifacts, myths, and rituals. Even the younger religions of the world still have mystical branches, such as Judaism's Kabbalism, Islam's Sufism, and Christianity's Gnosticism and its recent adaptation of Kabbalism. Thus, in addition to the emotional and psychological value found in performing

Rites, Ritual is one means of gaining direct access to the flow of creative energy (*qi*) that is ubiquitously recognized and engaged by shamanism and mysticism.

The concepts of a subtle energy body and the *chakras* are widely known today in the West. But many people probably don't realize that the concept of a light body, including in-body channels and spiraling centers of light can be found throughout shamanic and mystical traditions across the globe. In the West, we have become fairly familiar with the Sanskrit term "*chakras*" and the Chinese medicine system of acupuncture meridians, but many cultures other than these also recognize the body's energetic aspects. For example, Andean shamans refer to the light body as a light bubble (*poq'po*), the acupuncture meridians as "rivers of light," and *chakras* as "eyes" or "wells of light." Jungle shamans of that region talk of healing in terms of restoring our "Rainbow Body." The Inca flag that flies today in Cusco and throughout the sacred valley of Peru is the seven colors of both the rainbow and the *chakras*, and it reflects their cultural roots in the world of living light, the *kawsay pacha*.

Perennial wisdoms across millennia agree that this life force flows through the manifested cosmos, weaving a network of living energy whereby we are all interconnected and nourished. Hinduism and Buddhism recognize this web as Indra's Net, and the Peruvian shamans call this the web of creation, *tiqsi muyu*, or the *kawsay pacha*, meaning "the world of living energy."

This living network is the domain of subtle energy whereby the material world is manifested and sustained. What sets sages apart from others is the degree to which they are vessels of *kawsay*. What restricts *kawsay* are the damages, blockages and sludge that we accumulate through life experiences. In Peru, heavy disordered energy that clogs our light bodies is called *hucha*, and shamans work to clear away *hucha* in order to restore our Rainbow Body with healthy light energy. Healing, then, is a process of clearing and repairing the light body so that we are better vessels and transmitters of the living energy, by which we live and thrive.

An image of Indra's Net from Hindu mythology is that the world is woven from threads of living light. In the eyes between the threads, jewels are hung that are unique, reflecting in their facets all the other jewels in the net. Each jewel is the sum total of all the other jewels. Thus the whole is in each part and the part is in the whole—like a holographic image. We are jewels in the net and our highest form will bring us into harmony with this energetic network, giving sustenance to our own being while sustaining the cosmic web of life.

From the earliest of times, cultures across the globe have understood that we are children of light and form. The Earth is our Mother, accounting for our physical bodies, and the Sun is our Father, accounting for our light bodies. Like the Peruvians, the Hopi also believe we are children of the sun, and they annually celebrate with their Powamu Ceremony the living light that sustains Creation. The Sun is a manifestation of Great Spirit, and it is the Creator who infuses his love through the Sun to create and infuse the world with living energy—Spirit. Thus, to heal is to become a more impeccable vessel for the living energy of life, and to come into harmony with the interconnecting web of light.

Yet, luminous energy is not entirely ethereal, and it does have a subtle physicality—a vibrational frequency that can be perceived through our intuitive senses. It is influenced by sound, light, color, other natural elements such as essential oils and incense, and even our thoughts. Through the intentions and other stimulations created in Ritual, we can access the subtle world of living energy to clear and shift imprints that restrict or distort our lives.

The brain, as we know, also has various wave frequencies and brainwave states that are determined by the dominant frequency present. The *beta* state is the active, cognitive mind from which we primarily function (12-40hz). *Gamma* waves (40-100hz) are high during moments of insight or heavy processing. The *delta* state (0-4hz) is usually deep sleep or a deep healing state. The *alpha* state (8-12hz) is a light relaxation state that fosters creativity, intuition, and visualization. The *theta* state (4-8hz) is the deep relaxation state of meditation or trance and brings us to the edge of our unconscious. This *theta* state opens us not only to deep intuition and memory, but also harmonizes us with Nature.

The Earth's vibrational frequency of 7.8 hertz (called the Schumann resonance) is also in this theta range of deep relaxation. In *The Shambhala Guide to Traditional Chinese Medicine*, Daniel Reid explains that the Schumann resonance "is the ambient vibration of the planet, which constitutes the most important macrocosmic supersystem for the human energy system. This has been shown to be the most perfect frequency for healing and harmonizing the human energy system, for it permits the human system to resonate in perfect synchronicity with the pulse of the planet" (127).

The brain's frequencies are influenced by various stimuli including our personal emotions, thoughts, and patterns, as well as external forces, such as

1: Understanding Ritual

the time of day and sounds. When we are being creative or intuitive; or when we drum or rattle; when we sing, chant, or meditate; when we practice yoga or qi gong, or work with Ritual; we can bring the active mind into the alpha or even theta states from which we can stimulate natural healing and wisdom resources. When we immerse ourselves in a Ritual, quieting the mind and opening the heart, we can harmonize not only our brains, but also our light body with the healing rhythms of the natural world, and sometimes open the inner gateway (the *axis mundi*) to sacred dimensions.

It is apparent that you could benefit from Ritual without my ever addressing spirituality or the energetic aspect; so for those of you who prefer to stay on more solid ground, you may target the psychological and physiological benefits. Ritual works at multiple levels, and you can perform and tweak the Rituals to suit your time frame, beliefs, and comfort zone. Though, the more fully you can step into a mythic-mind state, embracing the possibilities of the intuitive mind, the more profound your Rituals can be.

Much of what has been considered "New Age," including sensing subtle energy, is really a re-awakening to ancient wisdom, and now even science is validating various aspects of such perennial mystical concepts. There are numerous excellent books with which you can delve deeper into the subjects I'm introducing here, and you can refer to the *Resources Appendix* for a few recommended titles. For our purposes though, it is enough to mention these basics and provide you with methods to gain some direct subtle experiences.

Sensing Subtle Energy

For those of you ready to deepen your awareness of subtle energy, you can perform the following exercises to practice sensing your subtle energy body—your light or your luminous body. As I discussed earlier, this luminous realm of your body, while both subtle and spiritual in nature, is still part of the material world—just at a very discreet level. In the audio-visual noise of our technological age, we may have lost our subtle sensory abilities, but we can begin to develop them again with practice. We can re- train our brains to see the auric field that surrounds all things or begin to recognize intuitive guidance when it comes to us via the gut or a general sense of knowing. The following exercises offer a good starting point for rediscovering your energetic field and your subtle *feeling* (touch) senses.

Healing Hands Exercise:

This exercise is a great practice for your subtle senses, but it is also an effective warm-up before Ritual or energetic work.

1. Rub your palms against each other briskly for about 10 seconds. Notice how they begin to heat up. Then, open your hands and notice the heat and any tingling that you feel along your fingers or palms.

2. Rub your palms together again for 10 seconds. This time, close one hand into a fist and open the other hand. Your full attention should go to the open palm. Try to feel a throbbing or tingling sensation. Notice any subtle sense of movement in your palm. There is a

1: Understanding Ritual

spiraling *chakra* in each of your palms, and when you arouse them, you might be able to sense their swirling flow. It's okay if you only sense the warmth or a throbbing at first; this is something you can keep practicing.

3. Rub your palms together again for 10 seconds. This time, when you stop, pull your palms apart by a couple of inches and try to feel the energy contained between them. For about 30 seconds, pulse the palms gently toward and away from each other, moving only a few inches in and out. Then begin to extend the distance out to about six inches and slow down the movement. As you pull out, try to sense the sticky feeling of the energy as it clings; as you push in, try to feel the slight pressure that builds. This is a gentle and moderately slow movement, but you must keep the pulsing action going or the energy disperses.

4. Building a Luminous Orb: As you continue to pulse your hands together, imagine building up a ball of energy in between your palms. You will start to feel the heat or tingling and some pressure as it builds. Remember, this is all very subtle and you may feel that you are imagining it, but keep on going until you can sense (imagine) its size and shape in your palms. When you have a ball about the size of a grapefruit, choose a part of your body where you have an injury or chronic pain and gently pull that nourishing orb into your body. Continue to pulse your hands over the area for a moment with the intention that you are continuing to infuse healing light. Do not think about the injury, only the pure healing energy that you are pulsing and its soothing effects on your body.

Perceiving Auras Exercise: *(This exercise requires partners.)*

Stand facing your partner, about 8-10 feet apart. Person A heats up her palms for 10 seconds, then holds up both hands in front of her with palms out. Walking slowly toward Person B, Person A holds the intention that her hands are "pushing" against Person B's field at chest level. Person B stands with his eyes closed, trying to sense when Person A's field presses against or into his own. When Person B feels something, he speaks out or puts up a hand. Person A can continue forward while both partners experience more subtle sensations, or you may quit as soon as Person B speaks. Switch roles and then repeat. If Person B doesn't feel anything, then switch roles, do the exercise, and then switch back and try again.

Note: Person A, though your thoughts are focused on "pushing," you might observe that Person B leans back or sways as you approach, even if he doesn't "say" he feels you. The body may feel the push even if the person does not sense the subtle pressure.

Enjoy playing with your luminous field. When finished, walk around a bit letting your arms swing freely forward and back, matching with the opposite leg (right leg, left arm forward, etc). This makes sure your circuits are flowing naturally and in the appropriate direction.

…

Contemplations for Chapter 1

1. In what ways have you sometimes felt that your life is missing depth or meaningfulness?

2. Recall a time when you have felt deeply in harmony with the universe, as if you were in sync with the creative life flow.

3. When have you sensed something with your heart, gut, or a tingling down your spine—something that you knew but could not have proven?

4. When have you given flight to your imagination and discovered something new?

5. What questions or wonderings have been aroused by the concepts of this chapter?

Notes

2: Creating Ritual

Sacred space is by definition liminal space. Because we are not in control and not the center, something genuinely new can happen. Here we are capable of seeing something beyond self-interest, self-will, and security concerns. True sacred space allows an alternative consciousness to emerge.
~ Ronald Rohlheiser (writing on Mircea Eliade)

Using the Ritual act, we can bring ourselves into alignment and harmony. We align our mind, heart, and personal will to a particular intent, and we harmonize ourselves with the natural world and its living energy. The nature of the Ritual experience is guided by its core theme or story that is woven by the mythic imagination from both archetypal and personal needs and beliefs. The imagination functions as a gateway or vehicle into a realm of opportunity for inspiration and transformation. When we enact a Ritual, we are stepping beyond ordinary space and time. We are creating an access point into a dimension of possibilities.

Anya – I have a need, give to me, you have a need, give to you

Tending the Soul With Healing Ritual

Spiritual Ceremony versus Ritual

Though we sometimes use the words interchangeably, it seems useful to make a distinction between the functions of "Ceremony" and "Ritual." In the spiritual context of our focus, both Ceremony and Ritual provide a connection to the Sacred and can foster a direct experience of the Divine. Both acts can be private or communal, simple or elaborate, and both can adhere strongly to tradition or be creative and unique practices. Furthermore, there can be ceremonial aspects to Ritual and Ritual elements or portions in Ceremony, as well.

Ceremony, however, has two distinguishing qualities. First, one of the key functions of ceremony is to honor or validate a person (or Divinity), or a special situation or event. Secondly, ceremony includes celebration or celebratory elements.

Ritual, in contrast, functions to create a *somatic* (embodied) engagement with the Sacred for the purpose of enacting change, or gaining wisdom or empowerment. Ritual does not necessarily have an implied celebratory nature, and it often can be emotionally or physically demanding, even leave one feeling challenged or exhausted. The deeper one goes into a Rite, the more one engages the power of the archetypes, and the more likely it is that one will face difficult truths that can draw sweat and tears. However, through Ritual, one often also finds surprising inner strengths, emotional balance, or a feeling of harmony within oneself and with the cosmos.

Michael Drake, author of *The Shamanic Drum*, explains the distinction well in his blog: "Ceremony is used to strengthen or restore the status

ritual doesnt have an implied celebratory nature

Ceremony - grounding
ritual - cause change

quo, grounding people in the natural order of things and/or deepening communal relationships. Ritual is a formal act or set of acts designed to cause a change in what is— to change or transform the status quo" (March 1, 2015 *Shamanic Drumming Blog*).

Invoking change within ourselves by engaging the archetypal forces that surround and infuse our lives cannot be taken lightly if we are to succeed. We need to respect the process and the forces at play, as well as our need to harmonize with the natural energetic flow that weaves us into reality. However, this does not mean we must be somber, sanctimonious, or overly stiff or formal during Ritual. Most of the Peruvian shamans I've known laugh frequently, often during Ritual. Along with a humility of spirit and a healthy respect for the awesome power of the Divine, we need to approach Ritual with an appreciation for life.

Opening the Axis Mundi

While we can conduct many moments in life in a more reverent and ritualistic manner, for the kind of spiritual Ritual work I am proposing here, you need to set your intentions at the *mythic* level: that realm of the unconscious and subtle domains from which dreams and myths come. This means targeting *more* than what your mind and heart can know. It means engaging the subtle realm of soul and seeking that mysterious benefit which is for a greater good. So, while you may perform a *ritual* with the intent to bring peace to your family, *Ritual* allows for more than the face-value issues to be addressed. By honoring the greater wisdom, by maintaining humble respect for how little we can know about the great mysteries at work, we come into rapport with the Sacred and

Tending the Soul With Healing Ritual

open ourselves to be empowered by the wisdom of that realm. Even if your desire is more practical or physically oriented—such as healing the body or a situation—your intent is to ask for this healing on multiple dimensions of reality and in keeping with the greater good. The "greater good" is simply that which is supportive of not only our needs, but also those of others and the living cosmos.

The difference between the Sacred and the secular or profane (meaning ordinary or non-sacred) is the abundant and harmonious flow of Spirit that infuses all that which is Sacred. We are each umbilically connected to the web of life through our inner channel, our *axis mundi*. The perennial wisdom of mystics and shamans tells us that to access the Divine directly, we must utilize this channel. This requires a certain state that allows us to bypass the protective constructs of the conscious mind and open to the power of the intuitive mind. The *axis mundi* then, functions not only as a channel, but also as a bridge or gateway that links us to the subtle realms. Mythology tells us the *axis mundi* connects us to the three worlds: the Upper World of Spirit, the Underworld of our inner soul and deep past, and the mystical elements of the Middle world where we live. Jungian psychology tells us that it connects us to our central Self and the collective unconscious.

For our purposes in these Rituals, it is most important that you are opening yourself to the realm of possibilities and that you let in the living energy that heals and balances. You may even find that drumming or chanting during your openings will help to soften your psyche into a more open and receptive state. Ritual helps us to mend and restore

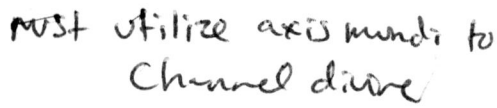

must utilize axis mundi to channel divine

our flow of energy and brings us into harmony with Creation, which is life-giving for each of us and for the whole of creation.

Five Components of Ritual

There is no mythic handbook to tell us categorically what we must do to engage the Sacred or how to make an effective Ritual. While many cultures still practice traditional Rituals, today there are also diverse ritualists who work with variations and remnants of extinct mystical or religious heritages. Moreover, some people create their own Rituals from their modern cultures. The five components of Ritual that I discuss below are based on my own research and experiences. After decades of personal Ritual work, as well as leading group Rituals in workshops and circle gatherings, I have found the following five elements to be essential for creating healthy and ethical Rituals.

#1 Working in Ayni

To effectively work with the realm of the Sacred, we must first establish rapport. The Quechua word, *ayni*, expresses the core relationship necessary to be in rapport with the Sacred. *Ayni* means reciprocity, and is often described as, "I give to you now and you give to me later, when needed." In Peru, an *ayllu* is a group of people who are in *ayni* with one another because they support each other by giving and receiving when there is need. We not only need to be in *ayni* with the Sacred, but also with others.

Ritual is not a device for imposing our personal will upon others, no matter how well-intentioned. When we impose our intentions into areas that are not under our jurisdiction, we inadvertently are committing an act of manipulation or *sorcery*. Sorcery, as I use the term, is an act (intentional or accidental) in which we overstep our authority. It is more than the obvious negativity of acting out toxic emotions. We are also committing sorcery when we presume to manipulate people and situations according to what we believe is best for them. Friends, parents, spouses, and even our children (after a certain age) are not ours to control at the level of soul.

Perhaps the hardest part of a spiritual life is recognizing that each person is on his or her own soul journey—one whose true purpose is unknown to us. If we over-protect or try to direct them, we can actually interfere with their soul potential. If we worry to excess, carry the burdens of their journey on our shoulders, we can interfere with our own journey. There is an art to both loving someone and accepting that they have a separate soul journey. There is an art to conceiving both the value of the individual *and* the holistic and inter-related nature of the universe. However, in Ritual, we can stand in that mythic realm between the worlds of form and spirit, and sometimes glimpse the truth of these and other mysteries in our hearts.

With this understood, you may still want to perform Ritual on behalf of your loved ones. You can always send healing and supportive energy to people, as long as you avoid imposing a specific outcome or agenda, such as, "he needs to move back home" or "she needs to change jobs." Therefore, to be sure your intent is solely for their higher good, perform Ritual first for your own healing, and only then for the healing or balance of another, by offering general positive support or healing love. Again, using the "highest good filter" is a great way to keep your intentions in check.

I list four other key elements for enacting Ritual below, but the most critical quality for working ethically and harmoniously with Ritual is to be in right relationship (*ayni*). Shamans know that when we are in *ayni*, subtle and mystical experiences can happen in the most unexpected times and ways. As your intuitive skills grow, you may find your subtle senses become stronger and more attuned, even when you are not in Ritual. Shamans also understand that the more you work with Ritual and build your intuitive power, the more accountable you become for reigning in that power—and staying within an ethical realm. So I encourage you to try to work from a state of mythic vision that sees beyond the obvious issues of the material and emotional realms and thus find the jewels and dreams that glisten in your heart.

#2 Reverent Intent

As you plan your Ritual, identify your heart-intent for the Rite, a deep-seeded need beneath what you can see on the surface. Beyond focusing on a superficial problem, try to understand the hidden undercurrents of the issues or changes that you face. When doing a Ritual for more general purposes—such as facing transitions in life or coming into balance—try to formulate your intent while leaving room for the Sacred to determine the "how." For example, instead of getting caught up in the details of what needs fixing, you can name the areas of concern and set an intent such as, "This Ritual is for bringing balance and harmony back into my life" or "This Ritual will help me release any residual angers or hard feelings that no longer serve me or those I love."

You may also wish to do Rites to awaken or heal an archetypal concept within you, such as the divine feminine or masculine, or archetypal elements in the world, such as Mother Earth. And, yes, you *can* do Rituals for more material purposes, such as healing a particular illness or wound, healing a relationship, balancing a particular circumstance in your personal life, or creating an initiation for a life transition.

Whether your Ritual intent is more general or specific, more spiritual or physical in nature, try to define what you need with words that resonate with power in your heart. Don't get overly philosophical, nor caught up in writing the "perfect" intent. However, do try to capture what you really need, as well as what would benefit others. So, instead of focusing a Ritual on "bringing your daughter home," you might set your intention "to bring your daughter close at heart." The difference here is that the first is a surface shift that changes her location, which may or may not create a healing. The second is your truer intent, for you and your daughter to become close again. When the hearts are close, you can bridge the distances, especially in today's world. Without getting too caught up in perfect language, write out your intent to help you think through your needs more fully. In the end, add the intentional tag "for the greater good" to help temper your own will with humility and leave room for divine grace.

#3 Sacred Space — Invoking the Numinous

If you are a Ritual novice, I recommend that you choose Rites from established, high quality sources (indigenous wisdom or resources with integrity). As you become comfortable with performing Rituals, you can modify them to accommodate your personality or needs. Once you have identified or designed your Rite and set your intentions, then you begin by creating (opening) a sacred space for the Ritual.

For less complicated Rites, this can be done with a simple honoring and prayer for guidance, protection, and the highest good. For more elaborate Rites, creating Sacred Space may involve Ritual preparations, such as procuring materials, cleaning or setting up a physical space, or creating an altar. All of the preparation should be done with a sense of reverent purpose.

Transforming ordinary space into Sacred Space involves creating a sacred process driven by your mythic intent. Through the processes of cleaning, organizing, burning incense, constructing an altar or a fire circle and other such acts, we are shifting the tone of an area to support us energetically. We become open to a *liminal* (in-between and transitional) space that bridges the material and spiritual domains—creating a translucence in the veil of subtle space-time.

Moreover, by going through the process of sanctifying the space, we accomplish our deeper intent, which is to open the fluidity of this liminal space within ourselves. By the act of preparing for Ritual and creating a sacred setting, we shift our focus from the conscious to the shadowy unconscious, from the rational to the intuitive, from the linear to the cyclical, from the material to the spiritual. We open an interior channel (*axis mundi*) and attune our hearts to the *kawsay pacha* (world of living energy—Spirit), and we direct our intent to the mythic, archetypal, and mystical Sacred. Carl Jung said that "For the unconscious psyche, space and time seem to be relative; that is to say, knowledge finds itself in a space-time continuum in which space is no longer space, nor time time" (CW Digital 481). This transitional space-time is where we can come into direct relationship with the timeless and placeless Sacred. Religion historian, Jonathan Z. Smith, explains that "A sacred place is a place of clarification (a focusing lens) where men and gods are held to be transparent to one another. It is a place where, as in all forms of communication, static and noise (i.e., the accidental) are decreased so that the exchange of information can be increased" (*Imagining Religion* 54).

In addition to clearing and preparing the external space, the act of creating Sacred Space facilitates an internal state of preparation and opening, which helps us to get out of our own way so that something wondrous can happen.

How to Create Sacred Space

Invocation — Calling In

The most basic necessity for creating Sacred Space is to request it. Traditionally, we call in the spiritual resources needed to work in Sacred Space. This prayer can be directed to the Creator, sacred spirits or energies, your higher self, archetypal forces, or whatever transcendent power that connects you to the Cosmic Sacred (*kawsay pacha*). You might call in nature energies, or power animals, or you might call in Angels, Saints, Christ, or the Buddha. The Creator has provided us with many sacred resources. We invite sacred energies and entities to help us thin the veils between the material and spiritual dimensions.

Honoring

Native Americans often call in the four cardinal or six holistic directions of the cosmos, recognizing the foundational forces that manifest life with living energy. However, they never ask without also making an offering, an honoring, to accompany such a request. Today people often exhibit an attitude of entitlement that humans have rights to take or use everything under the sun without needing to give something in return, or to even ask respectfully, with gratitude. In part, this may come from the idea that the world is an object, an inanimate place that we can exploit. However, in mystical, indigenous, and pre-science cultures, the cosmos is understood to be a vibrant ecosystem that we share with many living energies and entities. The planet itself is alive. They believe we need to honor those spirits and engage the reciprocal character of this holistic cosmos upon which we all survive. Only by giving something first in a stance of gratitude do we ask for something in return.

Burning sage or tobacco, pouring or spritzing flower (*Florida*) waters or wine, offering food, music, dance, drumming, or trumpeting a conch are some of the many ways indigenous cultures honor the Sacred. An offering of love and gratitude is made as one requests the presence of the Divine in order to keep us in *ayni*, right relationship. They teach us that one never only takes. We receive with one hand and offer something in return with the other. Thus, when we open Sacred Space, we want to do so with an honoring heart. When we call Spirit into our presence, we also need to be aware that we are inherently agreeing to come when Spirit calls us—this is the nature of being in relationship with the Divine, being in *ayni*. Opening Sacred Space, then, involves offering an honoring with our requests.

Guidance

After honoring the Sacred, the next step is to seek guidance. In asking for guidance we are really asking for the Sacred to be present and to hold us in divine wisdom. Whether we already know what is weighing on our hearts or are unsure of why we are coming to Ritual, we need guidance in our purpose and process. In addition to healing needs and initiation Rites, we can come to Ritual whenever we need to commune with or to work at the subtle level: the level of soul, subtle energy, and myth.

The perennial wisdom of shamans and mystics maps the mythic domains, and shamans-in-training spend decades learning the ins and outs of the subtle spiritual realms. Even the highest shamans rely on guidance from the Spirit world. We, too, need assistance from the higher Self, or whatever guides that we feel comfortable with inviting in to watch over our medicine work. Your guides can walk with you through your process and any mystical experience you might encounter. They can infuse your Rite with their love and support, help you to open your heart- mind, and basically help you to get the most from your Ritual. When we step into the Ritual as a sacred drama, we share the stage of this liminal space-time with the subtle domains. We can't truly be in Ritual without Sacred energies being present.

Protection & Boundaries

Though protection is implied when we request divine guidance, asking specifically for protection creates buffering boundaries. When we open ourselves up to subtle energies, we open to a dimension that has as many energetic personalities as the human race. Some fragmented energies are aggressive and needy and will want to attach to your light body. By establishing a protective bubble for your soul work, you create a filter to allow only the spirits and archetypes that are safe and supportive to be allowed in. Most of us have enough of our own energetic baggage needing to be cleared, we do not need to attract more.

The more focused you are on the sacred entities you want to work with, the more protected and embraced you will be by them, even if you cannot name them. You may ask to work with your personal spirit guides or power animals, even if you do not know them by name. When I'm not certain with whom I need to work, I may ask the Creator to send emissaries—but I am clear that they must be in the service of the Creator and the highest good. If you favor the language of depth psychology over spiritual terminology, you may ask to work with your higher Self and unconscious—your anima or animus, or particular archetypes.

A second aspect of protection is setting boundaries. By establishing the intention that only that which is for the greater highest good can occur, we set the intention that we are working with only sacred energies and only at that level that is for our highest good. It is important to set parameters for how much psychic energy can be accessed or released. If we open areas of our unconscious that we are not yet ready to face or heal, we can create psychological and physical stress that may overwhelm us. Why open floodgates when a controlled flow could nourish and heal us? Especially when we work on our own, without the guidance or support of a shaman or counselor, it is wise to move slowly and take precautions.

The safest way to practice Rites (and any soul work) is to come with desires and intentions, but to also acknowledge at the start that a higher vision and wisdom than ours should manage the process. We don't need to access what we cannot yet digest or assimilate healthfully. Instead, we come back again and again, whether for healing, initiations, or insight, accepting the pace and intensity set by a higher wisdom.

While all of this may sound complicated, in reality, a one sentence statement of intention can accomplish the goal. For deeper or more elaborate Ritual work, I enact a more elaborate opening prayer in which I name and honor the Creator and the six directions and their archetypes (S,W,N,E, Earth Mother, & Sun-sky Father)—calling them in and asking for guidance and protection as we just discussed. You can call in resources from a Native American or other indigenous or religious tradition that you respect, or you may utilize modern archetypal concepts of the Divine. For meditation and simpler Rituals, you can do a simpler opening. For example, you might light incense in gratitude and speak a brief sentence to ask simply for divine guidance, protection, and the highest good.

I like to rely on the "highest good" prayer as a way of not only protecting me from the awesome power held in the archetypal realms, but also *to protect the cosmos from me.* By placing my intentions within a realm of cosmic balance, I help myself to avoid over-reaching, as discussed in the *ayni* section earlier. I don't want to overstep my boundaries with my desires or needs. So again, by qualifying our soul work with the "highest good" prayer, we can step wholeheartedly into our Ritual, and still give voice to our heart's desires without worrying that we might be accidentally over-imposing our will.

#4 Ritual Drama — Engaging the Numinous

To fully activate the healing power of Ritual, we must step into the Ritual, in the same way you would completely embody a position in dance or a sport, or step into a role in a play. We cannot be both spectator and player. We cannot be fully *in* the Ritual and be questioning or analyzing it at the same time. An actress must throw herself into a role, and only evaluate the process *after* the curtain closes. Ritual requires a similar submersion—jumping in with full-bodied engagement, without thinking too much about the mechanics or whether something might seem weird or silly. I think of it as stepping in with *two believing feet*, and I personally learned this metaphor in a very concrete way.

The first time I ever walked barefoot across hot coals (at an Anthony Robbins workshop), I had not known beforehand that a fire walk was part of the weekend. A few hours into the event, when we found ourselves staring at the blazing bonfire that was to become our bridge to personal empowerment, I said to my husband, "It's going to take a lot more than a pep rally to get me to walk on hot coals."

However, several sensational hours later, I stood in line—both desperately afraid of *and* desperately wanting to succeed at walking that sizzling path. When my turn to walk across the burning coals came, I was determined. I made my requisite power move, and took my first step. However, surprisingly to me, I immediately felt a searing pain in my big toe that apparently burned out all the gray areas in my mind. I knew in that split second I had a choice to be all-in or burn. So as the saying goes, if you're falling, dive. I dove into the moment—all-in—and the second foot felt no pain. I walked the rest of the path without incident, though I was aware of the textures and smell of the coals burning in the sod pathway. I felt the rush of elation and a whole new perspective as I reached the other side. The path had been a bridge, and I knew that I could never go back to being the person I had been before. However, I did have a serious burn on the big toe of the first foot (the doubting foot) to nurse and contemplate. The second foot (the believing foot) was only blackened from the coals. When we step into sacred drama, we want to step in with *two believing feet*, because that's when the Grace flows and the magic happens! While the Rituals I describe in Part Two will not require anything so hazardous as walking barefoot on hot coals, every Rite should be entered with a belief in its possibilities for healing or transformation.

Every Ritual can be tuned for various purposes, but each has a particular mythic core that drives the Rite. For example, the sandpainting Ritual taught in Chapter Three is based on these mythic concepts:

- A mandala is symbolic art that can represent the cosmos or one's holistic Self;

- Working at this symbolic (mythic) level with the sandpainting can help to release, unfold, or shift perceptions and energetic patterns;
- The Earth nourishes us, mulches our waste, and contributes to our sandpainting work in a number of ways, such as holding symbolic energies in the natural components and absorbing the heavy energies or patterns that we release in the symbolic process;
- What happens in Ritual at the symbolic level can influence and harmonize the subtle and material patterns of reality.

By stepping into the Ritual, we step into its timeless archetypes and the sacred drama that it expresses. When we enact a Rite, we are embracing those mythic themes at the levels of mind (psychologically), body (somatically), imagination (intuitively), and subtle body (energetically). Healing Ritual is a creative process, much the same as the live performance of a play. Even when there is a predetermined script and setting, each rendition is a living, creative experience that is unique to all other performances. If a Rite becomes rote or solidified into static formality, it loses its metaphysical power and becomes a mere echo of the living thing.

The manner in which you open Sacred Space can help you get mentally prepared. Sometimes, I do a more involved opening process just to help me release the internal noise of ordinary life and step into the sacred art of Ritual. By setting up a space with decorative cloths, candles, incense, flowers and such, by singing in the spirits or doing an elaborate (not necessarily wordy) invocation process, my body and mind slide into a state of preparedness for the dramatic process to follow.

Part Two of this book offers a menu of Rituals to get you started. However, I suggest you treat my offerings as sample recipes, trying them and tweaking them until you get a process that works best for you or your particular intention. Remember, it is your Ritual: own it, enjoy it, be creative, and embrace wholeheartedly the gifts it offers!

#5 Closing Space

When you are finished with your Rite, pause for a moment to feel the resonance of the sacred setting. Feel the relief, the peace, the assurance, the clean sense of purpose, or the tingling sensations that are reverberating through your body. Realize that you are in a space and time different from the ordinary. Take in a deep breath, receiving the blessings that are offered. Let out the breath with a feeling of connection and appreciation. When you are ready, close the Sacred Space you opened for the Rite by offering gratitude and releasing the guides and the space back to the Cosmos.

You can do this releasing as a process that mirrors your opening, or you may close more simply. At a minimum, I like to say, "Thank you for your blessings and for coming when called." However, you can find your own words. When closing Rituals outside, you might like to leave something for nature, such as spreading nuts or fruit for the critters, or pouring water to nourish the plants.

I congratulate you for making it through the heavy theory portion of this book. It is important that you have some basic understanding of what Ritual involves and how to practice it safely and ethically. However, ultimately, to understand Ritual, you must experience it. I encourage you to plunge right into Part Two, where I believe a personal journey of wonderment awaits you!

Contemplations for Chapter 2

Take a moment to think about the current or recent patterns and trends of your life. Then think about the following questions:

1. What are the most common emotions that I experience regularly?

2. Are there certain patterns that seem to be playing out again and again in my life?

3. What would I really like to change in my life?

4. In what ways would I like my life to be better?

5. What physical or emotional obstacles could make it hard for me to use Rituals in my life?

6. What are some things I could do to get around or minimize those obstacles.

Notes

Part 2
Rituals Menu and Guide

> Everything depends on what is being enacted.
> Enactment itself, since it is almost synonymous with ceremony,
> is, as we have seen, part of the very fabric of our human life.
> We do enact things. We will enact things.
> No one can stop us from enacting things.
> ~ Thomas Howard (Evangelical is not Enough)

The menu of Rituals offered in this portion of the book covers a variety of purposes. You can perform the Rites as described, apply some of the suggested adaptations, combine them, or even revise them to suit your needs. As long as you are working in Sacred Space and stay in *ayni* with your intentions, these Rituals can be adapted to your personality and needs.

There are no particular standards for classifying Rites. So, to help you explore the mythic nature of these Rituals, I have grouped and explained them in archetypal terms according to their primary elemental qualities. Relevant mythic themes are reviewed at the beginning of each chapter to help you understand the archetypal (mythic) *and* energetic nature of that chapter's element and Rituals, and each Ritual is presented with a Theory/ Background section, when appropriate, to provide additional description or guidance. Review the material and instructions, then let the Ritual blossom as you bring it to life. It's okay to go non-linear now! At this point, you can continue to read in order or skip around to whichever Ritual section you are drawn to. (See the Rituals List Appendix for a detailed indexing of the Ritual components.) Let your mythic imagination flow!

3: Earth

The Nourishing & Swallowing Mother

The psyche and the cosmos are to each other like
the inner world and the outer world.
Therefore man participates by nature in all cosmic events, and
is inwardly as well as outwardly interwoven with them.
~ Richard Wilhelm, *The Secret of the Golden Flower*

The Great Mother is a force that both gives birth to creation and swallows it back up. She is understood to be the ultimate mother, bringing forth and nourishing life. Since perpetual increase does not allow for new life or ongoing creation, she must also destroy and mulch what is spent to keep nature in balance.

In the modern world, we seem to worship perpetual *growth* and *productivity*. Yet, to sustain itself, the life cycle must include rest and death. Instead of striving for incessant growth and expansion (as cancer behaves), we should strive for a healthy symbiosis. For a life to thrive, it needs a cycle that includes seasons of shedding, rest, and turning inward.

Mother Earth provides our food and resources, but she also swallows our waste and carcasses for mulching, recycling, and a return as new growth. She consumes the dead and the wasted so that something vital can once again be born and nourished. We want to come back into harmony with these natural cycles of life. Being in harmony with Nature is part of what Native American cultures refer to as "walking in beauty," or "The Beauty Way."

The heart of Peruvian shamanism is described by the Quechua term "*munay*," which means both "love" and "beauty." The love of the Creator is the source of *kawsay*, the living energy that gives life, and that divine love is manifested in the world as beauty. *Munay* is a divine love/beauty that suggests both inter- relation and divine order. This is the kind of love/beauty meant by "walking in beauty," such that we hold respect and affection in our heart for Nature and all life—as we live out our personal soul journey in the world.

When we work with Earth energy, we honor and value her nourishing aspects, as well as make use of her swallowing and mulching nature. Energetically, we need to restore our natural relationship with the Earth as a parent, and tap into her healing resonance. Not only can we reconnect with nature through Ritual, but we can also freely give her any heavy energies that need to be released. Our Great Mother's earthen body is made of dirt, ore, and stone, the heavier and more stable elements. This makes her a perfect and willing receptacle for heavy and disordered energies (*hucha*). We can comfortably release our negative, painful, or destructive emotions, patterns, and thoughts into the Earth and know that she will swallow and recycle that energy for the higher benefit. However, we are not shedding that energy in a state of hate or disgust, but releasing it to be revitalized. We should not hate *hucha* any more than we hate the breath we exhale. Instead, we can seasonally shed our old emotions and patterns naturally, as a snake sheds its skin or a stag its antlers.

Life situations stimulate the development of particular imprints or disruptions in our luminous field. These imprints tie us to the past. When old emotions or patterns hang on as festering wounds, they can become toxic to us and those around us. As with taking a fall on a muddy sidewalk, it is healthier to focus on getting our injuries cleaned and bandaged than fixating on the cause, embarrassment, or initial pain of the fall. Instead of prolonged rehashings of the event in layers of blame and upset, it better serves our well-being to take what lessons are available, get bandaged, and move on—keeping the lessons but not the mud (or festering wounds) with us. Ritual can help this process.

The Rituals described in this section focus primarily on the clearing and healing elements of Earth energy. However, the Harmony Ritual at the end of this chapter offers a nourishing attunement process that can be profoundly healing in itself.

Sandpaintings: Mandala Rituals

Theory/Background

Mandala is a Sanskrit word that means "circle." It derives its essence from the inherent symbolism of the cosmos, representing both the physical and metaphysical aspects of reality. Mythologically, the circle is a symbol for wholeness, and cosmic mandalas (whether simple or elaborate) depict a variety of cosmological archetypes. Eastern mandalas, as well as Native American Medicine Wheels, reflect the four cardinal directions and other astronomical, metaphysical, and symbolic aspects of the living Universe.

In psychology, mandalas are known to have appeared in dreams and therapeutic art. Carl Jung believed that mandalas represent the holistic psyche and can reveal hidden aspects or needs of one's true Self. The mandala altar Rituals described here draw from this image of wholeness, be it cosmic or personal. These nature altars are utilized as authentic and symbolic representations of your holistic Self, your personal Cosmos.

A sandpainting is a temporary altar that is usually produced outdoors on the Earth with natural elements and objects. The elaborate Navajo sandpaintings and Tibetan sand mandalas are examples of the more complex versions of this Ritual. By using intricate designs made from colored sands, they weave their spiritual intentions into the art form. The painting holds their prayers up to the Sacred for the brief but poignant and expressive life of the painting. Traditionally, when the Ritual is complete, the sandpainting creations are either dispersed or left to be disbursed by nature. The winds and rains sweep the makers' intentions away and into the Cosmos.

Our Ritual is a simpler version of this technique. You will create a mandala from natural objects that you gather and arrange. The Sandpainting process intentionally creates a temporary altar, the purpose of which is to activate a short term, but intense archetypal energy for healing needs. The goal is not to possess, harness, or stockpile these archetypal forces, since subtle energy, by nature, must flow to animate life. Instead, we want

3: Earth

to access the natural restorative flow through the channels that we open within ourselves, with nature, and in our sacred spaces.

Sandpainting 1: Clearing and Releasing

Description

Create a nature mandala with symbolic objects as a shedding and clearing Ritual. Your intention for this Ritual can be for general clearing, or you can target a particular aspect of your life.

Preparation

- Choose a relatively private or secluded outdoor location
- Gather natural objects (such as stones, sticks, flowers, or pine cones) to build a mandala

Ritual Process

1. Prepare for the Ritual and open Sacred Space. For this Rite, you may open Sacred Space before or after gathering the objects to use for your sandpainting. Personally, I like to make the finding and selection of the Ritual objects part of the Ritual proper, thus I open Sacred Space first. In either case, use your intuition to gather a collection of objects with which you will build your symbolic altar. Choose sticks, flowers, stones, seed pods, shells, or whatever bits that nature provides. You may also work with items that are good for nature, such as using dried fruit or bird seed to form your perimeter circle. You may want to use some personal symbolic objects in your mandala, but make the bulk of your

painting from natural objects. Just be sure to remove any personal bits once you close the Ritual—whether you dismantle it or leave your altar to dissolve.

2. Form a perimeter circle with natural objects, such as stones or sticks. As you build the circle, you are defining the domain of your medicine space and the Soul Self.

3. Choosing one object at the time, pick it up and literally blow an intention with your breath into the item. Look for unhealthy emotions, patterns, memories, attitudes, relationships and whatever you need to get out of your body and out of your life. You are *not* expelling the people, the gifts, or the lessons through this act. Rather, you are removing the related damaging energetic imprints that are stuck in your system. You're looking for heavy or disturbing remnants that weigh you down, that feel like unhealed wounds.

It is not necessary to remember each feeling that arises or what each object represents. You only need to let the sensations come to you intuitively as feelings, patterns, memories, or in whatever form they present, and blow these sensations into an object—releasing its weight and friction from your being.

4. After you infuse an item with meaning, place it somewhere inside the circle of your mandala. Build your nature altar one article at a time, blowing in the imprint and placing the item in the circle. Again, don't think too much about the placement; let intuition be your guide. As you work, you may feel like rearranging or stacking objects, and that's fine. You may also feel like blowing multiple memories or feelings into a single piece, and that too is fine.

5. When you have captured everything that seems to require attention, sit meditatively with your sandpainting. Let any memories or emotions that it arouses wash through you. If something still feels stuck, then add another item or add an intention to an already placed object. Follow any desire to move things around or make changes. Continue to sit with your mandala, radiating the intention that any *hucha*, heavy and disordered energies, are being embraced and held by Mother Earth. Let any remaining weight seep away and into the Earth, until you feel a level of clarity.

6. When you are ready, choose one final object to convey a deep feeling of gratitude and well-being. Now that you've released the heavy energies, tap into a feeling of appreciation for the gifts of experience and compassion that those old imprints provided. Also, enjoy the blessings of being able to let all this past clutter go back into the belly of the Mother to be mulched. Notice the strength of the Earth that supports you, and know that you have roots in the Earth and can release heavy energy any time you wish. Blow these feelings of deep appreciation into the object and place it into your painting.

7. Sit with your mandala until you are ready to leave it, and then prepare to conclude your Ritual in one of two ways:

A. Close Sacred Space and dismantle your mandala by scattering its parts back into nature—instantly ending the process.

B. Close Sacred Space with the wish that the mandala will naturally return to nature. This allows a gradual and natural closure to the process. Whatever feels right to you is the best to do.

Sandpainting 2: Mythic Mirror

Description

Create a nature mandala with symbolic articles as a way of drawing an energetic blueprint of your holistic Self and to stimulate a shift needed for healing or transforming a condition in your life. In contrast to Sandpainting 1, here you are not only trying to cleanse, but also to energize, balance, and heal various aspects of yourself.

Preparation

- Choose an appropriate outdoor location
- Gather natural objects to build a mandala

Ritual Process

1. Choose a specific issue or area of your life that needs support, balance, or just special attention at the mythic level.

2. Open Sacred Space and prepare for the Ritual. This process is the same as Sandpainting 1: Clearing and Releasing, except that your intention now is to shift a specific situation or pattern in your life.

As you open Sacred Space, set your intention to bring your target issue into your medicine altar for divine assistance. This might be a deep spiritual need or a more material one, such as an issue relating to health, finances, or relationships. You want to identify the core pattern or situation that needs work at the subtle mind and energetic levels.

3. Form a perimeter circle with natural objects. As you build the circle, you are framing a mythic mirror of your holistic Self as it relates

to your targeted situation. This mandala provides access to your subtle psyche and energetic dimensions.

4. As described in the previous sandpainting Rite, you will choose objects one at the time and blow your intentional focus into them, and place them into the mandala. However, in this Rite you are blowing in specific aspects related to your targeted issue. For example, if you are working on your marriage, you will infuse objects with qualities of the relationship and your needs. In addition to the key problems at the root of the issue, you might blow in your love, your desire to heal the relationship, your current feelings, or how you want to feel.

You may need to call in peripheral influences of other people or situations, such as job or security concerns or the needs of your family. As you call in the strands of issues and invite change, trust the Divine. Again, let your intuition be your guide. Don't get too caught up in the solution or reliving memories. As emotions arise, infuse an object and place it into the circle. Do this until if feels you have captured all the strands of the issue that seem active and relevant.

5. Now choose three more objects to infuse, but don't place them into the sandpainting quite yet. For these three objects, envision how you will feel when this situation is healed. You are *not* trying to envision a specific solution, but rather, specific benefits. That is, imagine the benefits of a healed situation. Imagine how you will feel better, happier, or more empowered when the situation rights itself. In line with our example, you might feel unrestricted love coming from your spouse, or you might feel excited about your future again. For a career issue example, instead

of imagining a specific employer or position, you can imagine what a better job would involve. Imagine how you would spend your time, the way people would treat you and how you would treat them, or how the improved conditions or pay would improve your life for the better. Think about how the healed state would feel in your life and inside you. Choose three primary images or image groups, and blow each of these empowered feelings into one of the three last objects—still don't add them to the mandala just yet.

6. Look at your sandpainting again, and using your intuition, without trying to think it, move things around in your mandala until the arrangement feels more orderly, beautiful, right for the healed state. It's like *Feng Shui* for your sandpainting. Stay in the poetic/mythic mind here. Let your intuition guide you into reshaping the energetic blueprint into a healthy pattern. Then, when it feels right, add your three power objects to the painting, wherever they seem to fit or bring the most beauty or balance.

7. Sit with your painting until you are ready to leave it, and then conclude your Ritual in one of two ways:

A. Close Sacred Space and dismantle your mandala by scattering its parts back into nature—instantly ending the process.

B. Leave your painting in place for a few hours or up to three days, then return to close Sacred Space and disassemble it. Don't worry if things have shifted or even disappeared in the interim. That's part of the mythic process too.

Extensions and Adaptations

Journaling

You may wish to capture some of the sensations or teachings that you gained from your sandpainting work, or delve deeper into some of the things that arose for you. Journaling is a great way to flesh out this material—as long as you explore it intuitively and don't try to over analyze it.

Journals can be done as writing, or as visual art, or a combination. As with journaling about dreams, rather than recording the details of your mandala or attempting to form logical connections and explanations, it is more important to capture your questions, perceptions, and emotions.

Adaptation 1: Indoor Altar

You can work with an indoor altar, instead, though I do encourage you to invoke as much of nature as possible by placing your mandala near a window, using natural objects, and scattering those objects back outside when you're finished.

Adaptation 2: Art Mandalas

If you choose to create an art mandala, you can do this, though this is a somewhat different process. Since the desire is to release or rework unhealthy patterns, you need to burn or bury the mandalas that represent the heaviness or significance of your problem-state.

For the Clearing and Releasing version of this Ritual, you can bury or burn your mandala as is. For the Mythic Mirror version, you will need to do two works of art: one that reflects the situation/pattern you want to change, and another that represents a blueprint for the healed or shifted situation. Burn the one that reflects the targeted issue, and keep the second mandala, if it feels empowering. Later, you may find you need to also let it go, so that you can envision something new.

Tip: Active and Passive Altars

Many of us have altars or Ritual spaces in our homes, even if we don't think of them as such. You probably have a shelf or mantel that holds special objects or memorabilia. These are indeed altars of a sort, but they are passive altars if we don't regularly utilize them in Ritual. You can certainly turn an existing altar into an active altar by performing Ritual with it. For my table altar, I keep a candle and incense burner on it. When I want to activate it, I open Sacred Space and light the candle and the incense. By opening Sacred Space and lighting the candle, I effectively "turn it on." I light the incense as an offering of gratitude before I assert my intentions or requests. For a mandala Ritual, you may want to utilize your entire altar space, or you might want to create a mandala space within it. I do this by having a round tray on my table altar where I sometimes conduct short-term indoor mandala Rituals. When you complete your Ritual, you need to disperse the items you used and close Sacred Space in order to release the energies, as you would with outdoor work.

Darkspring Khuya Ritual: The Clearing Stone

Description

Create a medicine stone *(Khuya)* to use for frequent personal clearing of heavy energies.

Theory/Background

Nearly every day most of us come home with some burden in our hearts. Whether we've had a specific conflict or bear general worries, these burdens can become sticky and clog our systems if we don't have a way to let them go. Some things cannot easily be drained, and we hold heavy emotions in various parts of the body including the heart, gut, or shoulders. However, even if the worry will not cease, we can learn to hold it in Sacred Space beyond our physical body. When we hold our burdens and wounds inside our bodies or subtle bodies, they can manifest physical symptoms, such as illness. This Ritual is a technique that I developed for myself and have recommended to many clients, especially those in service or care-giving careers.

This process activates a dark colored stone's absorbing properties. I call this the *Darkspring Stone* because it acts like a dark spring flowing deep underground into the belly of the Mother. Any heavy *hucha* we infuse into the stone is carried into the belly of the Mother for mulching.

This is a two-part Ritual process. The first part is a process for creating rapport with your stone, thus activating it as a medicine stone with healing properties. Once you have turned your stone into a *khuya*

(Quechua term for sacred medicine stone), then it will be charged for your daily cleansing Ritual.

Preparation

- Obtain a dark colored stone (not a crystal) that fits comfortably in your hand. Choose a dark stone that feels strong and comforting to you. It can be polished or unpolished, but it needs some size and weight in your fist.
- Gather a nice cloth, a candle, incense or sage, a bowl of water with a drop or two of essential oil or perfume in it, a small towel, and a pen and journal or pad of paper to write on.

Khuya Part 1: Awakening Your Medicine Stone

1. Lay out your cloth and place the candle and the stone on it. Include any other preparations you want to create for your Ritual space. Then light the candle and open Sacred Space.

2. Preparing your stone: Rinse it with the perfumed water to remove any dirt or *hucha*, then place the stone into the dish of water for several minutes and let it "drink" or "rest" in the water for a moment. Remove the stone and dry it off. Then wave the stone over the candle to symbolically infuse it with light. You are introducing the stone to two of its sister elements: fire and water.

3. Observe your stone closely. Notice its color and shape variations, feel its texture and weight. Smell the stone, and perhaps even taste it, if you like, to get to know the stone in intimate detail. Observe and learn all of its qualities and textures. Notice any images or thoughts it

triggers. Does its shape remind you of a bird, or does it have striations that look like rivers or mountain peaks? Try to grasp its nature physically and mythically. You want to become so familiar with your stone that you sense its unique identity and could even pick it out of a group of similar stones.

4. Next, tell your stone your story. Introduce yourself to it and tell it a little bit about you and why you need a medicine stone. Tell it about your trials, your family, your lifestyle, your job, or whatever seems relevant to how you will use the stone. Make the essence of yourself—your shapes, colors, textures, and dreams—known to your stone.

5. Now, it is time to listen to the story your stone tells. Your stone has lived on this planet for eons and holds a record of many stories in its shape, color, size, and its very substance. You are going to receive one of the stories your stone has to tell. Take up your journal and title the entry something like, "The story my dark stone tells." Meditate with your stone a few minutes to awaken the stone's story and to bring yourself in harmony with it.

Then, when ready, begin the story with this line: "Once upon a time when the world was young, I (*the stone*) had a _____ experience." Fill in the blank with descriptive words, then continue the story. You can make slight variations to this beginning, but keep it mostly intact, and absolutely keep the "once upon a time" fairy tale beginning. This is essential for activating your imagination. You are not trying to write a report of the stone's life. You are opening your intuitive senses to let the stone speak its story through you.

It may feel like you are pretending at first, but let the story unfold without over-thinking it. It may be a story about a simple occurrence, or it may reflect an epic moment in history or creation. Whatever the story is, it's important to just let the story come through you without second guessing it. Whenever you get stuck, you can write a lubricating phrase to get the juices flowing with this start, "What he/she wants to say next is something like …." and begin making something up. After a few words or so, you should find the story starting to slide through again. Your imagination is the gateway for your intuitive senses, which must be opened to communicate at the mythic level. If getting a story proves to be too difficult at first, at least capture any images or feelings that you sense during this process.

6. Now that you have connected with your stone at the intuitive level, bring your Ritual to a close by nourishing your stone with the air element. First, with your breath, blow your affection and appreciation into the *khuya*. Then smudge your stone with the smoke of the incense or sage as a final honoring. (Smudging means gently waving the smoke around and across an object or a person.)

7. When you are finished, find a place outdoors where you can safely leave your stone overnight to be balanced and energized by the Earth and all the elements. You might tuck it under some bushes or in the root base of a mighty tree. When you retrieve your stone the next day, be sure to close Sacred Space. You can begin working with it right away. Periodically, you may feel the stone needs clearing or re-balancing. When you feel it needs it, you can bring it back into harmony with nature, as described in step four of the Ritual Process section below.

Khuya Part 2: Using Your Medicine Stone

Description

Use your *khuya* to drain away heavy emotions and energies on a regular basis.

Theory/Background

At the end of the day or the week, or after a particularly challenging or difficult situation, you can let any heavy energies that have built up (in the form of difficult emotions, patterns, or ailments) drain away into the stone. Now that you have prepared the stone, it is ready to support you. You may need to recall memories to re-activate any heavy feelings and patterns so that you can then release them. Think of any events that have triggered debilitating feelings of pain, fear, guilt, shame, rejection or disempowerment. Look for those clinging emotions that feel as if the wound is still raw, as if the event is still current.

This does not suggest that everything hard that happens to you is damaging. Life is a process of learning and experience, and it will always be riddled with challenges and emotions. Anger and fear can be very appropriate at times, as well as important to survival or progress. A moment of guilt is a good reminder to keep us in check. But unhealed wounds and prolonged or obsessive emotions can putrefy and become toxic to us, as well as to others. Anger can turn to bitterness, old guilt can manifest as self-sabotage, and we can become suffocated by our own toxicity. Cleaning the various types of heavy emotions from our systems can be like clearing clutter, removing darts, or disinfecting wounds, and we can keep the teachings, the gifts, and the compassion that experiences provide without holding onto the injuries. The earlier we face these issues and release their imprints, the sooner we move beyond the wounds and their effects.

Preparation

- You can do this with as much or as little preparation as feels appropriate to you.
- If you choose to meditate with your stone, prepare a quiet place to work. The following steps offer a simple but effective practice, but you can enhance the process if you like.

Ritual Process

1. Keep your *khuya* in some convenient place—in your closet, on your personal altar, or even in your office so that you can use it daily or weekly, as you prefer.

2. Hold your stone and recall any lingering upsets or worries, any unhealed emotions, difficult patterns or memories that need to drain into the stone. Begin to recollect everything that still feels heavy, energized and clinging from the day, including the "would've, should've, wish I had" dialogues. What were you grumbling about to yourself on the trip home? What feels like it is hanging over you like a sword, clinging to you like muck, or smoldering inside like indigestion? What worries, fears, dreads, frustrations, or exhaustions are weighing down your heart, your mind, your body?

3. As you hold your stone, imagine the *hucha* of those heavy feelings as a dark cloud that moves from within your body down your arms and out the palms of your hands. Take a deep breath, then slowly exhale and imagine the fog moving out and infusing the stone, knowing the *khuya* will absorb and carry the heavy energy back into the Mother for mulching. You are not polluting the world or the Earth, any more than a deer pollutes the ground with his scat. The deer is fertilizing the earth with his waste. We feed the plants when we exhale, and they feed us when they exhale. Exhale your heavy energy into the stone, knowing that while it is waste for you, it is natural for the stone.

4. Though the *khuya* is charged to healthfully receive the *hucha*, over time you may feel that it has become saturated with disordered energy and needs to be rebalanced and recharged. Use nature and the elements to do this. You can nestle it at the roots of a tree, or lay it in the edge of a lake or out in the sun for several hours or overnight. While you do not need to open and close Sacred Space to use your stone, you do want to do so when you place your stone in nature to recharge. (Actually, I like to do the same for myself as well, using the Earth as a big *khuya*. I will lie in the filtered sun under a tree or on a shore and let any heavy energy drain from me into the ground.)

Harmony Ritual: Attune with Nature

Description

Perform a meditative visualization to attune to the rhythm of nature and be nourished from the flow of living energy (*kawsay*).

Tending the Soul With Healing Ritual

Theory/Background

Native Americans recognize that we are family with all of nature. However, people in Western cultures have been taught to separate ourselves from our nature relatives. Still, most of us have experienced moments of harmony or peace when we've been out in the countryside. We all know there are both psychological and biological benefits to being in nature. Part of the benefit is the way our bodies naturally attune to the rhythms of nature when we are in tune with it. However, for this Harmony Ritual, you will be going beyond the surface benefits to the body and mind. You will use your breath and visualization skills to more deeply harmonize your energy with nature for balance and nourishment.

Preparation

You can create a Ritual setting, if you like, but all that is necessary is to be in nature where you can experience the Ritual without interruption. You might do this in a park if you can resist being distracted by others. However, for the deepest work, finding privacy or solitude in a natural setting would be best.

Ritual Process

1. Find a place in a natural setting where you feel a strong sense of peace or comfort. Looking around, choose a prominent aspect of the landscape to be the focus of your Ritual. What tree or rock or stream or crest of a hill seems most comforting or captivating to you? Whatever geography or flora you choose to link with will become a "relation" during this process.

3: Earth

Settle down near your nature partner; I'll use a tree for an example. Open Sacred Space with a prayer for protection, guidance, and the highest good. You might make an offering, such as burning incense or spritz the tree with Florida Water.

2. Once you have created your bubble of Sacred Space, sit or lie down meditatively for at least ten minutes, mentally following your breath in and out. Use this process as a time to honor any emotions, worries, or memories that bubble up. Then hand them over to the Divine to manage while you let go. Release with each exhale any stress that rises in your mind or body. Do this until you begin to feel yourself relax.

3. As you continue to notice your breath, with the next exhale, follow your breath out and imagine that it is a cloud of nourishing energy that is infusing your tree. Now, as you inhale, imagine your relation is exhaling and you are receiving the cloud of its breath in your own body. Take it all the way in, letting the energy infuse you.

4. Continue this communal breath work, infusing each exhale with loving light as you imagine your breath flowing fully, into the tree. Then receive the loving energy from the tree when you inhale its energy. Try to stay with this until you to feel an attunement with your nature partner that instills you with a deep sense of peace and harmony with Creation.

5. After a while, relax your breath and imagine the energy moving between your respective centers. Imagine the heart of the tree beating in a calm but strong rhythm that calls to yours. Let your heart match its rhythm and the heartbeat of Mother Earth.

6. Release your body and your breath to these natural rhythms, and let yourself be swept up in the flow of the living energy into which

everything is interwoven. Imagine your heart open and relaxed. Notice the energy flowing between you and the tree as if you were energetically connected at the heart. Feel the constant flow of loving and healing light coming in and going out. Feel how sweet and nourishing it is to be harmonized with nature. Drink in this living Earth energy. Let it infuse your being with its vital luminescence.

7. Closing Sacred Space. When you are ready to begin closing this Ritual, once again, follow your breath with your mind. As you breathe out, send gratitude and farewells to your companion. While you were engaging nature, your subtle body will have expanded. As you breathe in, imagine pulling your subtle layers back toward your center. Do this with appreciation and joy, knowing that you can come back and commune with your tree at any time.

8. Come back to the material world by beginning to wiggle your fingers and toes. Take a couple of deep breaths, and then speak a closing that honors and releases the tree's energy. Hold on to that wonderful infusion of love and harmony as you journey back into your ordinary world. While sacred and ordinary domains are distinctly different, they can overlap, and we can continue to infuse our life journey with the beauty and light of spiritual dimensions. We can learn to walk in Beauty.

3: Earth

Notes

Tending the Soul With Healing Ritual

4: Water
The Purifying Elixir of Life

We can't help being thirsty, moving toward the voice of water.
Wash the dust from your soul and heart with wisdom's water.

Rumi

Mythologically, water is an aspect of the Great Mother and has many restorative and healing properties, both nourishing and cleansing. Unlike earth and stone, water is fluid and this fluidity makes water versatile in its gifts and uses. It is constantly in motion as rain and rivers, or as currents and waves. It readily yields to other forces, yet even a trickle can wear away a mountain or bring forth life in the desert. The human form is made up primarily of water, and shares the same fluid nature of the water that covers the Earth. The subtle nature of the light body is even more fluid, mutable, and versatile. Thus, Ritual can help us activate this natural fluidity to move, change, or go with the divine flow as needed.

For millennia, mystics have reported that both the human experience and reality itself exhibit a dynamic and mutable character rather than a fixed or concrete one. The Japanese researcher, Masaru Emoto, has done extensive studies in the pliable nature of water. His team exposed water to various influences, including prayer and intentional thoughts, emotions, and sounds, and they observed the resulting changes in the crystals formed when the water was frozen.

In his studies, Emoto took different sorts of water samples, some of which were very polluted, and exposed these samples to thought or sound stimuli. He then froze the water and compared the resulting crystal formations to those of the original sample. His studies demonstrated that, once exposed, there were changes in those crystallized structures such that samples with disordered or dull crystal formations produced beautiful snowflake-like structures. His resulting theory is that water can be influenced by consciousness and sound. Though Emoto's science is controversial, quantum physics has also shown that matter is influenced by consciousness, and other research projects from various fields are producing similar findings.

From Emoto's findings, we could surmise that our water-based bodies can also be shifted through exposure to thought and sound. This research implies that many of the concepts of reality and healing that have been practiced for eons by shamans, mystics, and a wide range of indigenous medicine men and women have gained scientific validation. Furthermore, Heart-Math, an organization that researches the intelligence and power of the heart, has shown that more information is transmitted from the heart to the brain than from the brain to the heart, suggesting we are not as brain-based as science previously believed.

Thus, scientific research is discovering not only the power of the conscious mind, but also the power of our intuitive wisdom, the Self or *heart-mind*. By heart-mind, I mean the sort of knowing that comes when heart-knowing and mind-knowing are aligned—an alignment that emanates from the deeper knowing of the intuitive self. In the Andean culture, to function healthfully and harmoniously in the world, we need to align our heart and head with our actions (will). This is how we are able to be in right relationship with the *kawsay pacha* (world of living energy) and to open up to the life flow for our own health and the betterment of the world.

Understanding the fluid nature of the body and light body, in addition to working with spirit guides, shamans use visualization techniques, sound, and Rituals to help people and their communities to heal and find the solutions they need.

There are various archetypal qualities of water, including nourishment and the quenching of thirst, the mythic river crossings required to move into a new dimension or world, the flow and currents that one can fight or ride, and the restorative nature of submersion, rain, and springs that bubble up from the ground. You can create many wonderful water Rituals that draw upon these various qualities in myths. The Ritual techniques in this chapter address three key aspects of water: nourishment, cleansing, and mutability (ease of change).

Rainbow Shower

Description

Turn your shower into a Ritual for clearing and nourishing the luminous body.

Theory/Background

This Ritual works with your *chakras*, which as we discovered earlier, are energy centers in the human body. They are about six to eight inches across and usually spin clockwise in the normal receiving mode (clockwise looking from outside your body). When the *chakras* are discharging energy for clearing, they move in a counter-clockwise direction. We will work with both directions here. These are your seven in-body *chakras*:

1. The root *chakra*, swirling downward from your perineum
2. The below the navel *chakra*
3. The solar plexus *chakra* between the ribs and navel
4. The heart *chakra*
5. The throat *chakra*
6. The third-eye, forehead *chakra*
7. The crown *chakra* swirling upward from the top of your head.

Preparation

Gather your typical shower accoutrements, and you may wish to play music, light a candle, or burn incense when you open Sacred Space in order to delineate the Ritual nature of this shower.

Ritual Process

1. Open Sacred Space in your bathroom. At this time, add music, candlelight, flowers, or other Ritual elements to transform the space.

2. First, briefly go through your normal bathing regimen, then begin the Ritual with Step three.

3. Discharge *chakras*: stand with your back to the spray and swirl one of your hands over each of your *chakra* areas in a *counter- clockwise* direction, beginning from the lowest *chakra*.

As you swipe your fingers in front of and around the *chakra* zone, imagine collecting any muck (*hucha*) and then rinse your fingers in the shower spray to let it be washed away. Open and swirl each *chakra* a couple of times, beginning from the lower *chakra*, working your way up to the crown *chakra* on the top of your head. For several minutes, stand under the shower and let the waters wash over you, rinsing your discharging *chakras* as they continue to clear. When you're finished, rewind each of your *chakras* in a clockwise direction to return them to a receiving mode, beginning with the crown and working downward.

4. Nourishing the light body: To further nourish the *chakras*, imagine your shower is a source of healing luminous water-light, streaming in the colors of the rainbow. Feel the seven colors flowing over your body, nourishing both your backside and your front as you move around in the spray. Then focus on one *chakra* at a time, nourishing each *chakra* with the color of its primary frequency. From lower to upper *chakras*: 1. Red, 2. Orange, 3. Yellow, 4. Green, 5. Blue, 6. Indigo, and 7. Violet.

For each *chakra*, imagine the water nourishing it with the luminous color associated with it. Visualize each *chakra* drinking up that water-light, quenching its thirst and nourishing its work. (There are light therapy systems out there, and you could certainly add colored light to your shower, but visualization is the most critical element of this process.)

5. When you are finished, feel all the rainbow colors washing over you once more, bringing light and balance to your luminous body. After you leave the shower, dry off. Close Sacred Space and sit or lie quietly, if you can, for several minutes to let the light continue to flow and balance before you jump back into the demands of the day.

Adaptation: Salt and soda bath

You can do a similar clearing and nourishing process in your bath, as well. Add salt and soda to your bath water, and do the clearing and re-illuminating visualization in the tub, imagining the tub water is a luminous pool of rainbow colored water-light. You can use whatever combination of salts you prefer, but this is my personal recipe:

2 cups sea salt, 1 cup Epsom's salt, 1/2 cup baking soda.

I find this mix alkalizes and nourishes the body and helps to draw out or neutralize heavy energies.

Florida Water

Description:

Make and spritz a flower (herbal) water, energetically enhanced to use for clearing and honoring during Rituals.

4: Water

Theory/Background

Florida is the Spanish term for flower and is commonly used throughout South America to describe the flower waters used in healing and cleansing Rituals. The Florida Water commonly used in Peru is mostly made of alcohol and various essential oils with a wonderfully strong flower scent. As introduced earlier, luminous energy has a subtle physicality, and its frequencies can be influenced by sound, light, color, movement, emotion, as well as both the scent and energetic properties of herbs and flowers. Florida Water is a great tool for clearing spaces, opening Sacred Space, and for clearing objects, and your own body of heavy energy. Any time you have the desire to clear a space, clear your own field, or make an offering, you can use Florida water.

More than just cologne, it is traditionally spritzed by shamans from the mouth, carrying their healing intentions. However, you can put it into a spray bottle if you prefer. If you do not want to make your own, you can buy Florida Water from shamanic websites or from sites that sell blended essential oil or Pranic Healing sprays. Be sure that whatever you use, you energize it with your intentions.

Florida Water Recipe

This is my personal recipe for Florida Water, but feel free to change out the herbal/flower essences for various purposes or your personal preferences. However, the stronger the herbal and flower essence, the more strength the water has, so be careful not to make it too mild. Also, let me point out that if you want to spritz by mouth, you should make your water <u>only with tinctures or essential oils that are safe in the mouth</u>. If you put your water into a spray bottle, I recommend using essential oils to get as strong an essence as you can without muddling the scent.

Preparation

Basic Recipe Ratios

- Two parts high grade vodka
- One part strong green or herbal tea
- Flower and herbal tinctures or Essential oil drops to achieve strength and balance
- Mixing pitcher and bottles

Making Florida Water

1. Steep an herbal tea, such as green or white tea, for several hours or overnight until it is very strong.

2. Add one part tea to two-parts vodka in a glass pitcher or bottle. (I like to use clear stopper-top lemonade bottles). You can use a little less vodka in proportion, but it is easier to spritz by mouth with more vodka, and the vodka serves as a preservative.

3. Add dropperfuls of tinctures or single drops of essential oils until you find your right balance. I make a larger bottle of the mixture, and then use it as a source to fill smaller bottles. When working with tinctures, start with two or three droppersful of sage, and add about half that of peppermint. I keep going until I get the strength and balance that I like. Then I add drops of other tinctures or oils to bring depth and complexity to the flavor and scent. Use whatever you like according to

your preferences and herbal knowledge. This is an intuitive process. Since I spritz by mouth, the flavor is my guide. However, if you will be using a sprayer, let the scent be your guide.

4. Infusing Your Intentions: Choose a word or short phrase that represents your intention for this water, write it clearly on a piece of tape and attach it to the bottle or pitcher. Choose words or phrases that are clear, such as "health," "clarity," or "joy." Holding the bottle, imagine infusing the contents with your intentions. This can be done by speaking the word or phrase with emotion, by singing or chanting to it, or by just silently visualizing the thought or feeling you want to infuse. Wake it up, make it strong, give it a purpose.

5. If you have a shelf or table altar, you can place it there. If not, then make a simple but beautiful altar on which to place your pitcher for steeping. Keeping Emoto's findings in mind, choose a beautiful place in your home, and place crystals or objects that have great meaning for you onto the altar. Though you want to make the space meaningful, keep it uncluttered since you want the water clean and bright. Open Sacred Space for the altar, and leave it to steep for several days. You can stop by each day to re-infuse the water with your healing intent while it steeps. You may further wish to infuse your water with sunlight, starlight, or moonlight by developing your altar outdoors or near a window. You can play music, sing to it, surround it with flowers, or add colored light to its setting. Let your heart guide you.

6. After 3-5 days, close your Sacred Space with gratitude. Dismantle your temporary altar if you made one. You can transfer some of the water into a smaller bottle if you made a larger amount, but keep the large bottle

in a nice, cool place in your home (not the refrigerator or bathroom cabinet). Keep it on your shelf or table altar if you have one, or keep it in a special place.

7. Spritzing by mouth: When you spritz, you tip the bottle to get a small amount of water in the front of your mouth. You are not letting it get fully into your mouth, but just at the tip of your tongue. As soon as the water is in your mouth, spray it out with tightened lips to disperse it lightly into a mist. This does take practice, and sometimes you dribble. The key to good spritzing is taking small amounts and keeping it in the front of your mouth. The value over spray bottle spritzing is that when you spritz by mouth, you are infusing your intentions with your breath.

So, for example, if I am clearing my office before I sit down to work, I am letting the Florida Water help me to act out my intentions. My intentions infuse the water and the water manifests my intentions. I'm working mythically by working at the physical *and* at the mental and subtle levels. Spritzing with a bottle is still valuable, and I do have several bottle blends that I buy or make. Still, to me it seems to be one step removed from the power of your intentions. I especially like to mouth spritz as an offering when I open Sacred Space or for deep clearing. You need to do whichever process feels right to you. Remember, energy follows intention and attention. So though the flower essences bring certain qualities to your water, focusing your intentions is the most important factor when using Florida Water.

Ritual Uses for Your Florida Water

Clearing Space and Objects

As mentioned, you can use your Florida Water to clear and balance spaces and objects at any time that you feel it is needed. Not only do the vibrations of the water act upon the space, but the act of clearing can help you to psychologically and energetically release residual emotions. You can similarly clear a space in your home before or after activities or company. Take the attitude that you want your space or object clear and balanced, not weighted down with heavy energies. When you spritz, imagine any *hucha* being swept into the belly of Mother Earth where it can be mulched and recycled. (You can also add Florida Water to the bowl of water for the Darkspring Stone Ritual in Chapter 3).

Clearing People

The water can also help you clear residual energies from heavy emotions or encounters. As with objects, imagine that the fog or sludge that still clings to you from heavy emotions or situations is being swept away and into the Earth as you spritz yourself or others. Clear with an attitude of bringing into balance and restoring right relationship. Be careful not to add any negative attitudes, anger, or judgments. You just want to clean what isn't healthy or supportive.

Getting messy is part of living. Clearing your energy body should become a normal part of your personal hygiene. If you are a care-giver—whether medical, psychological, emotional, or energetic—you will benefit from having techniques for clearing yourself regularly. It is difficult to care for others without getting a little involved with their issues or absorbing some of their heavy energy. Your feelings of empathy can create energized connections that make it easy to absorb *hucha* from those you mentor or care for. It is a good idea to clear yourself regularly, not from a place of fear or disgust, but with the same pragmatic attitude as you would wash your hands after tending a wound: cleansing, non-judgmental, and practical.

Honoring

Florida Water is aromatically pleasant, and therefore, it is a perfect offering to the Divine during Ritual. By honoring the archetypes and the forces of Nature and the Cosmos, we create a rapport—a relationship founded in respect. The prevalence of an attitude that the cosmos is somehow subservient or inferior to humanity and our needs creates discord between us and the natural world. Yet, many traditions do recognize the necessity of harmony between humans and nature. For example, Peruvian shamans take few actions without first honoring the life-giving forces in the world: Upon waking, before eating, traveling, planting, or making decisions about life. This is *ayni* when we come into a symbiotic relationship, rather than taking on an attitude of entitlement and exploitation.

When opening Sacred Space, you can make offerings to the Sacred and natural world in a variety of ways, since the key is to show respect. Traditionally, music, food, drink, medicinal herbs, and incense have been the primary offerings. Ritual is not to be confused with the idea of sacrifice. This is not about owing or buying some favor by paying a fee, especially one of discomfort. It is about showing respect, just as one would to a friend or neighbor with whom one lives in relationship. If I need to borrow a cup of sugar, I don't go to my neighbor and demand it as my right. I respectfully request the sugar and offer my gratitude for that gift. Inherent in that exchange is the understanding that when my neighbor in turn needs eggs, I will happily provide them, with joy at being able to reciprocate. This is *ayni*, the relationship we need with the cosmos and all life on Earth. And, it can start with how you interact with the people and the archetypes with whom you have a relationship in your life.

Blessing

You may also use your Florida water to help you bless spaces and objects. It is wonderful to bless a new home, a new car, and new things that are important to your life personally or spiritually. I have held small blessing ceremonies over every car owned by a member of my family for decades. A blessing ceremony can be as elaborate or as simple as you desire. When I bless my home, I create an elaborate process that includes playing music, burning incense, and walking through every part of the house first smudging with the sage and the intention of clearing. Then I walk through with gratitude and ask for blessings as I spritz Florida water throughout. It is good to honor not only the house, but the land, the neighborhood, the town, the region, and the world—all of Mother Earth and the bounty that gives us life.

Adaptation: Qi Drinking Water

You can infuse your drinking water with intentions, just as we did the Florida water. Fill a glass pitcher with drinking water. Write a word or phrase on a piece of clear tape and stick it onto the pitcher. Holding the pitcher, infuse the water with the properties you wrote on the tape by visualizing your intentions for it. In addition to the Ritual procedures described above, you can add slices of cucumber and lemon, or whatever you would prefer. Be sure to keep it in the refrigerator if you add fruit or vegetables.

Reflection Pool Ritual

Theory/Background

Many of us have been taught that too much self-love can be dangerous: it's narcissism. Narcissus, of Greek myth, obsessively adored his reflection pool image until one day he dove into it and drowned. However, it is not self-love that destroys Narcissus. It is self-worship. It is not healthy to love oneself above or to the exclusion of all else. Yet, a healthy love of self *is* important, even essential, to being able to give and receive love fully.

This Ritual draws once again from the theories of quantum physics and Emoto that suggest consciousness can influence reality. Since our bodies are mostly water, and since our cells are ever replacing themselves, our bodies are not fixed in their current state. For this Rite, we are using a mirror as a healing reflection pool to send love and intentions into our own fluid bodies. We need to re-open the dialogue of who we are and how we want to be, shedding the past that has become fixed in our body's appearance and function. Whether we want to heal problems, feel and look healthier, or get out of ruts in which we find ourselves, we can empower change by re-opening the dialogue with our inner sense of Self. This isn't about returning to some ideal of youth, but rather nurturing the Self with love and imagining our best Self in the present. We can learn to re-configure the blueprint so that we change who and how we are becoming.

Description

A visualization Ritual to restore a healthy dialogue with your Soul Self, opening you to self-love, healing, and personal evolution.

Preparation

A mirror that is large enough to see your face and shoulders, clear packing tape, a permanent marker, paper and pen, and any setup you desire to make a pleasing Ritual.

Ritual Process:

1. Open Sacred Space and whether you are working with a bathroom mirror or working with a smaller mirror, create a beautiful setting for this Ritual. You might want to play soft music during the meditation portion of this Ritual.

2. Look into the mirror for several moments and briefly note what you don't like. This might include physical critiques, a general distaste for

how you look or how you behave, but just take a quick stock of what you don't like about you.

3. Looking away from the mirror, take about one minute to list on your paper some of the things you would like to change. Think about how you would like to be, or how you would like to feel when you look at yourself in a mirror. Avoid unattainable targets of "perfection," and negative overtones like "be skinnier" or "look younger." Choose words that hold a suggestion of excellence (not perfection) in the word, such as "fit and beautiful," "energetic," "compassionate," "to love and be loved," or "healthy heart." Keep it brief, using key words and phrases only.

4. Now, looking over this list, decide on up to three words or phrases that *identify the qualities you most want yourself to embody or possess at this time.*

5. Write those words or phrases on the clear tape and stick it to the mirror just below where you see your face reflected.

6. Now, gaze into the mirror and look into your eyes. As you connect with yourself, periodically say the words you stuck to the mirror. Look at the words, look at yourself, and begin to feel what those traits or changes feel like in real life. This is a meditation that should not become too busy. With "soft" focus, quietly look at yourself and look at your words. As you say the words, feel the possibilities, and look again upon yourself. Sustain this mirror meditation for at least fifteen minutes.

7. After this meditation, when you are ready, you can take the meditation deeper. This can be difficult at first, but it will get easier with practice. Look into your eyes for a prolonged period (blinking is okay but keep a soft focus on your own eyes) and send love to your reflected self.

As you see love reflected in your eyes you may feel waves of emotion. Allow the love you send to also be received by yourself. You may find yourself moving between being the lover and the loved. Stay with it. You may also feel tears or discomfort, but stay with it. The greatest emotional deficiency most of us experience in life is that of self-love. You may have to repeat this Ritual many times to be able to sustain this self-love meditation for more than a few minutes, but try to hold your eyes for at least five minutes the first time. Once you learn to recognize and receive love from yourself, it will become easier to recognize and accept the love of others.

8. Close the Ritual and Sacred Space when you are ready. You can continue to support your changes by taping the words on your bathroom mirror, inside your kitchen glass cabinet, or other places to remind your psyche of who you are becoming.

Like Emoto's water crystals, you are sending messages to reshape your patterns and molecules, and you want to keep sending and receiving the positive intentions over an extended period of time. If you feel the need for significant changes, I would encourage you to do the full Ritual daily for about a week, then at least once or twice a week for several weeks or months.

Tending the Soul With Healing Ritual

5: Air

Wind, Breath, Mantra

*I am never alone wherever I am. The air itself supplies me
with a century of love. When I breathe in, I am breathing in
the laughter, tears, passions, memories, existence, moments,
and the hues of the sunlight on many tones of skin;
I am breathing in the same air that was exhaled by
many before me. The air that bore them life.
And so how can I ever say that I am alone?*
~ C. JoyBell C.

Mythologically, the element of air has several primary characteristics. In its still form, it represents the invisible and life-sustaining essences of Creation, particularly spirit and soul. As breath, it reflects the life force that moves within us, and the term *qi* can be translated as air, breath, and energy, as well. In the Hindu culture, *prana* (the life force) cannot exist without *vayu* ("air" or breath in our bodies).

Wind is the moving form of air in the world, and it can be gentle and comforting or it can bring violent storms and change, sometimes shifting without warning. The four invisible pillars of creation, the contrary forces that meet and comingle to create the cosmos, are called the four directions or the four winds. Cosmic mandalas reflect these creative forces and the archetypal qualities associated with each of them.

Humanity participates in creation by accumulating and channeling *qi* through our breath, words, and thoughts. Our breath helps us to move *qi* and channel our thoughts, and there are many ancient practices for using the breath not only in silence, but also with sound and movement to create health and to manifest desires. Various Eastern traditions, such as yoga and qi gong, utilize breath and movement to cultivate and channel *qi* for health and holistic well-being.

In this chapter, I offer two such Ritual breath and movement techniques that can be done by nearly anyone. However, for those with experience, you can adapt the Ritual qualities here to more advanced yoga or qi gong movements. These can make wonderful practices that you can use to begin your day with gratitude and joy, and come into balance with the universal flow.

Sun & Moon Salutation

Description

A light yoga series that uses breath and intention to greet the day, and bring flexibility, flow, and balance to mind and body.

5: Air

Theory/Background

This can be done in the morning, evening, or both. This Ritual works in several ways. It helps us to open our hearts with gratitude, and it helps connect us with the living cosmos (nature) which is both healing and comforting. The Rite also oxygenates and moves our body for suppleness and energy flow, and we begin to re-discover how to move *qi/prana/kawsay* again. This Ritual is best done outdoors where you can be exposed to the sky and earth, but you can do it wherever you are able.

Breathing Note: If you are having trouble with the breath timing, it's okay. The most important thing is to keep breathing. Generally, inhale when you open your chest, and exhale when you contract or compress your chest. The idea is to breathe gently and deeply as you move.

Preparation

You need a place to stand and greet the day, outside if possible, or near a window. It is not necessary to open Sacred Space here, because this whole process is a kind of Sacred Space Ritual. However, if you desire, you can request protection, guidance, and highest good.

Ritual Process

1. Stand with your feet slightly apart, with hands in prayer position at the level of your heart. Close your eyes, seat your awareness in your heart, and briefly ask the Creator to hold you in Sacred Space as you greet the day.

2. Open your eyes, reach your hands up to the sky and greet Father Sun and your sky relations. Continue holding your arms up as you side

bend to the right and then to the left. (At Night: honor Grandmother Moon, the Stars and Planets, and your sky relations).

3. Spread your hands wide, sweeping them in a swan dive down to the ground just outside your feet, bending your knees as needed, and greet Mother Earth and your earth and sea relations.

4. Place your palms on your shins and straighten your back. Then hang loosely and greet your body, feeling your feet planted and your body folded into itself.

5. Roll your back up, returning to a standing position, inhaling through your nose. As you come up straight, stretch your arms out into a wide outreaching—even behind your body a bit—and arch your back slightly with your face uplifted. Greet the day or night as a gift, taking several breaths.

6. As you exhale through your mouth, gently sweep your arms forward, closing/crossing them over your chest, and lower your face forward. Inhale and draw the gifts of the day or night into your heart, knowing that you are receiving divine love and living energy.

7. Keeping your feet planted and your left hand on your chest, twist your torso toward the right, and gently sweep your right hand behind you, resting your knuckles against your left hip (or as close as you can comfortably reach). Breathe in and out of your nose several times, being aware that your feet are grounded to the Earth and your stationary body is active with energy. Twist forward and return your right hand to your chest.

8. Now do the same move on the left side. Exhale as you twist your torso left, sweep your left arm behind you, take several breaths, and feel

your body in harmonic resonance. Release your breath and the twist, returning forward.

9. Inhale as you sweep your arms back, out, and up to the sky in a reverse swan dive. Then pull them back down with palms together at your heart. Exhale and feel the energy moving through your body. Relish the joy of the moment. You can repeat this series as many times as you like.

10. To close this Ritual, I recommend that you say three Om's out loud to calm and stabilize your mind before you rejoin daily life. Your Om should be drawn out for the length of a slow exhale, leaving the "O" open until you near the end. Then close the "M" and taper off to the end of your breath.

Why Om? "Om" is a Sanskrit seed sound that carries no word meaning, but rather is used for its frequency. In Eastern practices, Om is said to clear our minds and open us up to the formless and timeless reality. Energetically, Om helps to attune us to the Earth's frequency, which is the healing theta frequency discussed in Chapter One. Physiologically, the sound resonates through our system, calming our minds while bringing energy to our bodies. Studies have further shown that a regular practice of Om stabilizes the nervous system.

Adaptation: Drinking the Light

If you want to take this Ritual deeper energetically, you can hold prayer position and drink in the light energy of the Sun or Moon through your belly. Send your attention down to the area just below your navel, and imagine the *chakra* swirling there in a clockwise spiral. Now imagine that spiral reaching outward and opening up to let in more light. When it feels expanded and wide open, imagine the nourishing light drawing into the *chakra* and infusing your body with beauty and light. The act of drinking the light opens your body to receiving energy, thus allowing it to recharge naturally. When you are finished, imagine your *chakra* drawing back into what feels like a comfortable size.

Walking Mantra Meditation

Description

This is a meditative movement coupled with an intention-based mantra to help shift change at the energetic and unconscious levels. While this is a form of meditation, by opening Sacred Space and having a specific reverent intent, you are creating a visualization Ritual.

Theory/Background

This is a movement meditation Ritual that integrates concentrated intention with breath and movement. When we couple movement with intention, we activate our intuitive wisdom, including heart and cellular intelligence. When we use the meditative mind, we can engage our subtle energies as well, and therefore shift patterns at the level of body, deep mind, and light body. Though it is most effective when done daily for a period of time, I never discourage sporadic practices since any time spent in Ritual is supportive and beneficial on several levels. There are two actions for this process. The first is the meditative movement, and the second is the mantra. Once you learn these processes, as always, you can personalize them.

Most people are familiar with sitting meditations, practiced either in silence or with mantras to quiet or direct the mind. While I have practiced such forms of meditation for decades, I have also long been a fan of movement meditations, including qi gong and tai chi (a form of qi gong). Surprisingly to me, my first experience with a simple walking meditation took me to an unexpected depth of meditation and awareness. I do not necessarily advocate movement meditation over others, but rather value varied techniques depending on one's purpose or state of mind. If you have trouble with sitting meditations, you might find this Ritual especially refreshing.

Movement serves several purposes. First, it gives the mind something to focus on at the start of the meditation, which helps to quiet the banter of surface consciousness. After a short time, the movement becomes automatic (unconscious) and your mind can settle further. Second, by pairing a mantra with the movement, your intention is infused through both the somatic and energetic bodies. As a circuit of breath and movement is created, you are engaging the body and the mind, as well as moving energy. This way, the intention becomes known to our entire selves, encoded into our brain, heart, cells, and *chakras*. Third, the repetitive nature of the Ritual coaxes us into a trance-like state in which we get beyond (or upstream of) the level of mind and body, and attune to the theta frequency of the Earth where we can affect true change and healing through intention.

Preparation

- Comfortable clothes
- A location where you can move and speak undisturbed, preferably outside.

The Movement

For this Ritual, you take slow, shallow lunge steps, as if you were stepping on stones in order to cross a river. The steps are neither normal lengths nor deep lunges, but rather slightly extended or reaching steps. Beginning from a stable position, step out with your right foot and let your left (opposite) arm sweep out and form a slight curve in front of your chest. You will be speaking your mantra as you step. As you release your arm out and down to your side, inhale and begin the next step. As you step forward with your left leg, lead with your right arm, curved into a crescent shape. You can pause briefly between steps or let them flow continuously at a slow and gentle pace.

Notes: Be sure to inhale before you step, and exhale into the mantra so that you are breathing out your intentions, as well as letting them resonate within you. You can adapt the movement style to suit your needs, but use both your arms and legs and keep the movement gentle and fluid so that energy keeps flowing. The object is to keep the energy and breath moving, to stay focused on your intent, and to sink into the deeper realms of Ritual. If at some point the mantra drops to a whisper, or becomes silent, that is perfect too.

The Mantra

Theory/Background:

Mantras are sounds used in Ritual and meditation. They may be non-thought oriented, such as Om and other Sanskrit seed sounds found in Eastern sound meditations, which are used primarily for their mystical or frequency values. Other mantras, in contrast, are succinct statements of belief or intention that can help us to make shifts or focus intentions at the subconscious and soulful levels. As with fine art and poetry, the less rational and more poetic we are with our mantras, the more our soul-mind can align with it. It can help to be specific, but keeping our intentions at the mythic level allows for possibilities and divine assistance we might not imagine for ourselves.

Mythologically, belief, often termed faith, is understood as an essential vehicle for gaining a direct interaction with the Sacred, as demonstrated in these examples. Jesus is quoted in the Gospels as having said that healing came through the strength of one's own faith, "Did I not say to you that if you believe, you will see the glory of God?" (John 11:40). In the Buddhist hymn of faith, the Avatamsaka Sutra states that, "Faith is the source of the Path or Way. Faith is the mother of merit and virtue."

Thus, when we write an intentional mantra, we need to approach the intention from an organic core of belief, rather than from a typical agnostic core of disbelief—a "try it and see what happens" or "seeing is believing" stance. Philosopher and Islamic studies professor, Henry Corbin, asserts succinctly that modern Westerners have to bypass the ingrained "agnostic reflex" in order to be able to engage the intuitive and mystical aspects of reality. To access intuitive power and divine gifts, we need to step into a "believing is seeing" approach, with two believing feet.

In practice, this often begins by pretending a thing is true, the way a child pretends. When a young boy pretends to be a tiger, he steps fully into his idea of "tiger." In his mind, he joyfully becomes as much of a tiger as he can animate for a few minutes or sometimes days. Like the child, we want to learn to pretend so well that for at least a few moments we are wearing a fully believing heart. In his novel, *Life of Pi*, Yann Martel also seems to suggest Pi's imagining of himself as a tiger may have unleashed his hidden strengths for survival. When activated by imagining, our psyches open up to the subtle domains engaged by Ritual. This can clear restrictions or blockages that we may unknowingly harbor. I do not suggest we can single-handedly change the whole world or even get everything we want, but rather that we can help manifest what we need at the Soul level that supports our lives and the living cosmos. Still, we are allowed to ask for what we want and believe we need, while we also honor the harmony of the Universe and the wisdom of the Creator.

You can use the much-loved Om seed sound for this meditation, as it has powerful therapeutic qualities. However, I also recommend more involved mantras. Though I will give you a few sample mantras, you will want to personalize your mantras to your needs. For a mantra to tap the creative power available to us, it needs to be more than a wish. It needs to be a statement of reality empowered by belief, clarity, and gratitude. I encourage you to begin doing this Ritual with spoken mantras. However, once you get the hang of it, you can whisper or silently think your mantras for this process, as well.

Writing a Mantra

Your mantra may be a poem, a chant, short phrases, or longer statements. Just be sure that it is short enough to memorize so that you can transcend the physical process of recalling the words in order to achieve a meditative experience. Longer mantras may need to be spread over multiple steps to keep the flow going. Though it may feel stiff at first, you'll find your rhythm.

Be Positive and Believing:

Achieving power with the Divine hinges on two key factors:

1. Being in right relationship (*ayni*) as discussed earlier, and

2. Choosing a state of believing from which to approach the Divine.

Frame your mantra in belief, as a truth that is already reality or that is a reality in the process of becoming. Choose language that is positive, believing, grateful, and that relishes the Universe's desire to conspire on our behalf. You may have to start by pretending to believe, but when you keep imagining, moments of real belief will slip through.

Use words and phrases to focus your mind on your goals and dreams, not on the pitfalls you wish to avoid. If you wish to safely cross a narrow rope bridge (or a bed of hot coals), the key factor is to not look down. We need to imprint intentions, not avoidances. Just as the "Don't think about an orange" immediately triggers the thought of an orange, a negatively phrased mantra can highlight and possibly activate what you do not want. Instead, the phrase "Think about a monkey" turns my mind and emotions in an entirely new direction, and the orange is forgotten. Instead of "I want a job without a jerk for a boss," a mantra that includes "a new and enjoyable job where my talents are appreciated" creates a link to what you want. Or, instead of saying, "I want my back to stop hurting," the sentence, "My back is strong and supports my passion for tennis," will turn your attention toward new thoughts.

In the world of subtle energetics, we say it in this axiom "energy follows attention and intention." This means that where you focus and how you direct your intentions has the power to influence the course of your life. We are not sole-creators; thus, our intents are part of a pool of energetics that weave a consensual reality into being. However, if we do not take an active role, we let others create reality for us.

We are co-creators of our personal and greater world. If there seems to be a lot of bother in life, we must recognize that we may be unintentionally inviting in or somehow participating in what's happening. Whenever we see a negative recurring pattern establishing itself, we should consider the possibility that we may be assisting that pattern with our limiting thoughts, feelings, or beliefs, or by being a bystander in our own lives.

Be specific, yet also, be mythic. It is important to design mantras clearly, identifying your desired outcomes, yet always also allowing for the greater insight and possibilities of divine wisdom and power. Try to hold your needs in the realm of infinite possibilities and focus on the benefits you desire (good relationship with your daughter), rather than the characteristics or symptoms (she will stop arguing with me). The beneficial result—not the how. You want to be clear, but do not try to micro-manage the universe. An important aspect of clarity is using active wording that you can visualize. Abstractions cannot be embraced by the body-mind as fully and deeply as images. Consider these two mantras:

- *I am getting better every day in every way.*
- *I am becoming more healthy and cancer-free each day.*

These mantras are positive, but they could be more potent. They do not give clear images of what "better" or "healthy" actually is or feels like, and the second calls attention to the diseased state. You need to focus on the true target and step into the belief that healing is an accomplished fact or at least an active process, so that the body-mind can begin to learn and embrace this truth. Wishful thinking or a "trying" mentality, does not embrace an actual outcome. The following mantras offer a clear image of what has been accomplished or is currently happening in the body.

- "I feel healing energy flowing through my body, nourishing and rejuvenating every cell." (In process, but draws a clear image to be embodied now).
- "My heart is whole and I am strong, fit, and joyful today."
- "Each time I think of _____, I feel a healing wave of compassion and forgiveness flow through my heart."

What if you just don't know what you need, or how to ask? Surrender is often the very best thing we can do. Here's a sample mantra for when you cannot be specific, don't know what to ask for, or are just feeling overwhelmed. When we give over control to the Sacred, we can get out of our own way. This opens us to divine assistance and allows our natural healing processes to go to work.

Here's a sample for surrender.

> "I surrender to Divine care. I know that I am loved, and that I am worthy of the blessings and bounty that are, at this moment, being created for me."

Ritual Process — Putting the Parts Together

Now that you understand the parts, let's put the Ritual together. Open Sacred Space by becoming present and reverent in your heart as you would at the start of a meditation.

1. Stand with your feet apart, palms together at your heart, and draw your mind to your center. Feel your feet connect with grounding Earth energy, feel the crown of your head connected with light energy (the Sun or Night Sky), and feel a sense of your authentic Self in your heart. This is an alignment of the above, the below, and your center.

2. Take several breaths in this position to become fully present, and speak your mantra several times to be sure you have it.

3. When you are ready, step forward with one foot, circle your opposite arm out, be sure to breathe, and adjust your body and motions until they feel natural. As you move into the step, begin your mantra.

4. Lower your arm, inhale, and take your next step and continue or repeat your mantra.

5. How long you do the Ritual is up to you, as long as you stay in it and aren't making errand lists in your head. I recommend at least thirty minutes minimum at a time. If your mind does flit off, it's okay—just pick up the mantra again and refocus. You can use more than one mantra in a session, but I recommend staying with one for at least 10 minutes before changing.

6. When you are ready, come to a hands at heart position and close Sacred Space.

Frequently Asked Questions:

Q. Does this mean I can manifest anything I want?

A. Yes and No. You can manifest anything you "truly" want at a soulful level, and which is in harmony with what the Divine wants, what the living cosmos needs, as well as what is best for you. Never doubt that we are being parented by Spirit and our higher Self, as we would direct and protect our own children. We are loved and the Universe wants to help us, but our desires must be balanced with our needs, and the needs of the rest of Creation.

Q. Can I create mantras to help others?

A. Yes and No. You can absolutely create mantras to send intentional love, healing, and support to family, friends, and even world leaders and big businesses. Just be careful. When you start writing a mantra that your daughter will dump her boyfriend or your boss will resign or get transferred so you can have her job, you are crossing over into intentional manipulation. This is not being in right relationship.

Q. Will I get better results if I do the mantra meditations several times a day?

A. If it comforts or feels healing to do it twice or more times a day, then do so—but be careful. What makes this Ritual powerful are the depth of your belief, the clarity of your intention, and the gratitude and state of being in right relationship with the Sacred. Frantic repetition, desperate pleas, and anxious wishes do not empower you. These are fear-based desires, and they carry little power when uttered from our weakest Self. It takes balanced repetition to build psychological and energetic space within ourselves to make room for Divine possibilities. Practice your mantra work in a state of calm and trust. Imagine that when you perform the Ritual, you are placing that prayer in a cosmic inbox where it will be addressed. Each day you weave the threads of its truth inside you, as well as offer it up for divine support.

Mantra Templates

Just to get you started, here are a few more samples, and some basic templates. Use words and phrases that evoke strong images or emotions for you.

Sample of mantra for specific healing (sight):

Day by day, my eyes see with more clarity, and my heart sees with more love and beauty.

Sample for clearing:

Divine love is, at this moment, dissolving and eliminating everything unlike itself in me. I am whole and enjoy life.

Sample Template:

I embrace the blessings of _____ and _____ that are even now creating _____ in my _____.

Adaptation: Walking a Labyrinth

Walking a labyrinth is a form of walking meditation that awakens our non-linear nature. By winding through the spiral, we are taken beyond the linear "to and from" mindset. We wander in circular patterns that weave us to a center and back out. Just walking the design can profoundly shift our mental and energetic patterns. However, you can add a mantra or the meditative gait used in this Ritual to your labyrinth walk for a deeper experience.

I prefer to speak a mantra on the journey in toward the center, then pause for reflection at the center, and walk back out in silence. Chanting, singing, drumming, rattling, and dancing are also wonderful ways to experience a labyrinth.

If you want to do a labyrinthine walk without a labyrinth, you can add curls to your path such that you turn and loop around as you work your way toward some generally determined center spot. Then curl your way back out. A labyrinthine meditation is a good way to remember that the journey to Spirit is deep, not far.

Tending the Soul With Healing Ritual

6: Fire
Alchemical Transformation

*Man is a thinker. He is that what he thinks.
When he thinks fire, he is fire. When he thinks war,
he will create war. Everything depends if his entire imagination
will be an entire sun, that is, that he will imagine himself
completely that what he wants.*

~ Paracelsus (1493-1541)

Like water, fire has mythologically been understood as a transformative element. Both water and fire purify and renew—water by dissolution and fire by transformation. However, where water also nourishes, soothes, and has a primarily feminine character, fire destroys. Whether fire consumes a thing to ash, like a stick of wood, or whether it transforms a thing, like sand to glass, the original substance is usually changed beyond recognition. Fire is a masculine form of transformation and is understood in terms of not only heat and flame, but also light and enlightenment.

Some gems of wisdom we pick up along the way, like stones upon the path. Other forms of wisdom slide over us like a cool breeze or into us like a refreshing drink of water. Still other types of wisdom come to us in a disturbing torrent of heat that can disorient, cripple, or even kill off a part of ourselves. Thus, direct experience with the Sacred can come as a rush of heat and energy, and it can inflame our own passions and sense of purpose.

Death is a key component of fire, as the fuel that feeds it must be consumed. Transformation requires the letting go or casting off an old form or pattern so that a new and revitalized pattern can emerge. This is the alchemical transformation that turns lead into gold, or in more mystical terms, the *prima materia* (the first or basic matter) into the ultimate substance called the philosopher's stone. Peruvian shamans understand that in fire, wood turns to ash and the light entrapped within it is released back into the world. This reflects the process of personal healing and transformation, as well. They understand that for healing, we need to release the heavy *hucha* to be mulched by the Mother, so that the light (our light and the flow of living energy) can once again flow freely and healthfully. Transforming Rituals allow us to burn up or break up damaging imprints and patterns, so that our light bodies can heal and we can be returned to a balanced state.

Fire Ceremony

Description

A personal or communal gathering at a fire, with a personal healing Ritual process. A fire ceremony provides a beautiful process for asking for

6: Fire

and receiving blessings, and for releasing heavy emotions, attitudes, and beliefs that are blocking our healing.

Theory/Background

This ceremony uses fire to burn away the *hucha* that needs shedding, but releases the gifts as light and smoke. When we burn a stick, we let the heavy matter turn to ash and keep the gifts of those experiences. The first time you do this, I encourage you to perform the Ritual as described below for a general healing of your past. See it as an opportunity to shed all the dead skin of old events, feelings, and beliefs that no longer serve your well-being. However, you can also use the fire ceremony to target specific issues or patterns in your life. You can do this Ritual alone or with others. When you have a group fire, each person still approaches the fire individually to do his or her own individual work, while others hold space together. Holding space could include singing, drumming, or thoughtful silence.

When you can, it's rewarding to build an actual campfire for this Ritual in a fire ring. However, you can scale this process down by building a mini-fire in a heat-resistant bowl, or even smaller by using a candle or incense. I explain the candle/incense variation as an adaptation below.

Preparation

Gather small to medium sized firewood, starter kindling and sticks, olive oil, small sticks for Ritual, and aromatics such as sage, Palo Santos, or incense. Be sure to have water on hand for safety.

Firewood

Stack a few sticks of firewood near your fire ring before you start. You don't want to choose huge logs since you want the fire to burn down to a safe pile of coals before you leave it—both for safety and to be sure the work of your Ritual fire is complete. I suggest setting up a small starter mound of fast burning material in your fire ring with additional kindling and small sticks, along with your larger firewood nearby.

Ritual Sticks

Also gather small sticks or flammable bits of nature to use for your Ritual work and stack these beside your fire pit. For a first healing fire, you may need fifteen, twenty, or more sticks, but later, when working with narrow and specific topics three or four may be enough. Let intuition guide your choices.

Ritual Process

1. When you feel you are ready, return to the fire site, and open Sacred Space (if you haven't already). Teepee several logs over your starter mound before you light it. Feed the starter mound with more kindling and larger sticks until your firewood catches flame. Continue feeding it until your fire is going strong.

2. As your fire matures, in a spirit of gratitude and honoring, make one or more offerings by pouring olive oil onto the burning wood. This feeds the fire and makes another offering for *ayni*, in preparation for your medicine work. This Ritual can be conducted in silence, or you may wish to chant or drum while you wait for the fire to become "friendly." This

is also the time to focus your intentions in order to release any old and limiting beliefs, feelings, or whatever else bubbles up. What dead skin do you need to shed? What do you want to change in your life? What do you need to bring into your life?

3. When the tallest flames begin to settle and the fire is more approachable, it is time to begin the active part of your Ritual. Sitting or kneeling in front of the fire, let a feeling or memory come to mind and then blow the emotion or thought into the stick. You are using your breath to expel any heavy thoughts, memories, or regrets that arise. Then place the *hucha-* infused stick into the fire to burn. Remember, you are shedding the heavy *hucha* associated with that memory or emotion, but you are still keeping the gifts, by releasing their light from the heavy matter. With one feeling-infused stick at a time, keep shedding and burning until you feel clear.

You may feel shudders run through your body or tears flow. You may experience specific images and memories, or you may not even know what you are feeling or why you might be crying. It does not matter whether you know what specifically you are blowing into the stick—it only matters that you keep blowing any feelings or sensations into them until it feels as if you are done — at least for this round.

4. Periodically, when you have several sticks burning, reach over and draw the gifts as light and smoke into your heart. Imagine that you are pulling in the gifts and teachings of those memories, even as you are releasing the heavy *hucha*. These gifts are already yours, and you won't lose them if you don't do this, but this movement can help you to value and re-embrace the blessings of past experiences. You don't want to do

this (or any) Ritual in a state of disgust or hatred. It's about recognizing there is value in all of your past, while releasing the aspects that are not supportive.

Some of your thoughts may be very good ones, but you still need to blow them into the sticks because there is probably still something that needs healing or perspective. For example, a fond memory of your grandmother may bubble up, but you blow it into the stick anyway because what you may not realize is that a bit of unhealed grief over her death is sitting as a heavy imprint in your luminous field. Trust the process. Trust the wisdom of Spirit and your inner self.

5. Once you feel you are finished with the Ritual, place an aromatic offering of sage or incense into the fire, adding your gratitude to the gifts of smoke and aroma for the Cosmos.

6. *Integration*: To help anchor the healing, before your sage offering has completely burned up, draw the smoke into your body at three points to anchor this state of *ayni*. First, pull it into your belly with an intention for walking in right action (service). Then pull it into your heart *chakra* for right feeling (love). Finally, draw it into your forehead (6th *chakra*) so that you will walk in right knowing (wisdom). The concept is that when our personal will, heart, and mind are in alignment with the conscious universe, then we can walk and live in our sacred purpose—in Beauty.

Right action is living out this wisdom and love in the world through an attitude of service. It's an attitude of willingness to work and to help others whenever we can. *Right thinking* is knowledge and wisdom drawn from our inner and higher wisdom. *Right feeling* is approaching the world and others from a place of love and understanding—a perspective of caring about the whole, not just our part of it.

In Ritual, you have come to a sacred liminal (threshold) state where you stand between the physical and mystical worlds, and where you can shift things within your being at subtle and spiritual levels. While in Ritual you can feel the love and support of the Sacred host: divine guides and angelic beings. You can feel the presence of your deepest Self that belongs to this sacred cosmos and that has a purpose in life. But to make a difference in your life, you need to keep some of this with you as you move back into your daily world. This last part of the Ritual helps you to anchor those feelings of connection, divine purpose, and inner wholeness, even as you leave Sacred Space.

As you pull the smoke and light into yourself, imagine Divine love, wisdom, and strength infusing your being. Know that you are always connected, and that you carry these gifts with you back into the ordinary world.

7. Sit for a moment, to anchor the blessings of this Ritual. Close Sacred Space by thanking the Divine for protection, guidance, and the many blessings.

Adaptations: Candle/Incense Variation

You can use a small fire source, like a candle, in which you would use very small items to burn, such as a twig or a sage leaf. Then, when it is nearly burned, set the twig or leaf into a fire-safe dish or bowl so that it can finish its burning. For this variation, you will do fewer items. This is better for working with particular issues in which you will only need to burn a few prayer sticks. To do a big shedding Ritual, you really need to build at least a small fire outdoors.

For daily or lighter work, you can open Sacred Space, light a candle, and blow your issues into pieces of incense. Then, let that incense burn. Sit with it as it burns and imagine continuing to release heavy thoughts and feelings around your particular issue.

When the incense is getting near its end, draw the smoke into the solar plexus, heart, and forehead *chakras* (as we did with the fire ceremony) to keep the gifts. Remember with this act you are drawing the gifts into these *chakras* as you release the heavy parts.

Close Sacred Space and blow out the candle once the incense has been consumed.

Fire Breaking Ice Ritual

Description

A Ritualized act of destruction to help you healthfully release anger and other *hot* emotions.

Theory/Background

Sometimes we want to move past an event, but just can't seem to shake the residual anger or bitterness left behind. Other times we get stuck and cannot seem to break out of a pattern. One of the shadow sides of living in a civilized and well-mannered culture is the repression of certain of our human inclinations, our base instincts. Sports is one of the few activities where we can freely act out aggression or some of our violent urges. Our culture stresses the value of constructive behavior, but it makes little room for destruction and deconstruction—cycles that we know are equally important in nature. As a result, most of us repress at least some of our *hotter* emotions, encasing them in restrained behavior and beliefs in order to conform, to survive, or to keep the peace. They are like fire trapped in ice, buried and bound without the cold and rigid walls we've built in our psyches. In this Ritual, we safely chip away at those icy barriers, freeing some of the heat and life-force imprisoned by icy control.

In his book, *The Mythic Imagination*, Stephen Larsen discusses a client's dream that reveals this exact image:

> *A woman who seemed frozen in her ability to resolve certain problems of life dreamed about a snow-covered volcano. I asked her to indwell the volcano....What emerged was an impression of enormous heat and power, slumbering under an icy exterior. The image from nature showed exactly the state of the psyche. She needed to contact and release the heat within her in order to overcome her icy impasse (84-85).*

Breaking the ice can help us to release the suppressed anger and other *hot* or debilitating emotions or patterns without having to explode or implode from the pressure. However, it is vitally important to do good journaling work before and after this Ritual, to be sure you are giving voice to the force so that it can continue to disperse.

To make this more than a temper tantrum, this must be done from a mythic place, with the best intentions for healing—yours and that of others. Without the mythic encounter through Ritual, though we might benefit from acting out our anger, we cannot get to the upstream energetic realm where we need healing. Be aware that this Ritual is not intended to replace therapy necessary for psychological trauma or anger management. It also may not be appropriate for persons with anger or abuse issues. Instead, this process is structured to help people deal with typical issues faced in common circumstances in life.

This Ritual is designed to help get those imprints out of the liver, heart, or wherever they have taken root in your system. This does not replace the need to work through your problems on the material plane. However, clearing out some of the debilitating energy may allow you to better understand problem situations and to better communicate with those involved.

Preparation

Find a place on your porch, driveway, or in your garage where you can safely do this activity. Find a board or surface that can take pounding. Half fill one or two one-gallon zippered heavy-duty freezer bags with ice cubes. Leave the bags of ice in the freezer until you are ready for them. Get a hammer or kitchen mallet. Have your journal near you.

Ritual Process

1. Pre-Ritual Journaling: Think ahead about what needs to be purged energetically. What are the hotspots in your heart or belly? What memories, circumstances, or people trigger fury, bitterness, resentment, or even a sense of hatred? You probably already know the main imprint that

needs venting, but if you have several, you can work this out on paper before you get the ice out of the freezer. You can work on this even days before the Rite, but the key here is to uncover the issues, and admit to your feelings.

2. Open Sacred Space and think about what you want to ventilate in this Ritual, naming your intentions either silently or aloud. Remember, you are not venting upon or at anyone or anything. Rather, you are ventilating your system by giving your emotions an outlet, through your actions.

3. Place a freezer bag of ice on your pounding surface, and when you are ready, begin pounding the ice with your mallet. Let yourself enjoy the sheer pleasure of this liberating act of destruction.

4. You might also vocalize while you're breaking, to further release emotions, such as rage or unexpected waves of elation. You might dedicate some of your strokes to certain thoughts, feelings, or attitudes, saying things similar to these: "This is to release my fury" or "guilt." You can also exclaim words and short phrases like "no more," "freedom," or "enough!"

5. As your poundings activate a release, the process may also awaken other emotions, such as elation, empowerment, relief, or forgiveness. There may be a range of emotions. Whatever bubbles up is okay, just let it wash through, like waters under a bridge. Check yourself if you start directing your anger or negative thoughts toward individuals.

If one bag of ice is not enough, break another. When you feel finished, you are finished. You may feel the kind of exhaustion that follows moments of big emotions or you might just wind down to a calm and balanced peace. It will depend on the nature of your emotional work, but trust that whatever the experience provides is what you needed.

6. Close Sacred Space: for this Rite, it is especially important to close Sacred Space with more care than usual. You need a more distinctive transition from this time of sacred destruction back into a world where you must be more civilized and careful about what you say and how you behave. It's not okay to walk back into the kitchen and start breaking plates because the dog scattered the garbage. This Ritual only works if your destruction is held in a mythic container.

Do a careful closing, being sure to come back to a place of gratitude. Then take the ice remains outside and pour them around a tree or bushes so that the heavy energies can be mulched by Mother Earth. Pour it out with good wishes for the part of nature that will benefit from that water and heavy energy.

7. Three Oms: To help leave the emotions of this Ritual in the mythic dimension, after you have poured out the ice and closed the Space, say at least three Oms to resettle your mind and heart. Speak each Om with a slow exhale. Hopefully, your Ritual will bring you back to a peaceful state naturally, but if you feel agitated, you should continue to Om until your mind and heart feel settled.

8. Post-Ritual Journaling: Now that you have completed the process, within 24 hours of finishing the Ritual, you need to go back to your journal to debrief and integrate the process. Describe the most important happenings during the Rite, how they felt, and what realizations they triggered. Once you've captured the things that seem most critical, then turn your journal writing into a letter to yourself. Acknowledge

6: Fire

the emotions that you unleashed, and find the gifts/teachings that they brought with them. Determine which counter-emotions will help you to continue to release them: forgiveness, self-forgiveness, compassion, joy of life? Choose one or two balancing emotions to practice in your daily life, as a continued healing process.

Notes

7: Conclusion
Beyond Reason

*This current world of ours would appear to be
physical, sociopolitical, and economic.
But our sixth sense—the imagination—discerns another,
which shines and streams through cracks in our visible universe.*
~ Stephen Larsen, The Mythic Imagination

My primary intent for this book is to provide opportunities for fellow soul-tenders to rediscover their intuitive senses and to reconnect with the luminous realms of the Sacred. Through Ritual, we can develop our intuitive senses, rediscover our centered Self, reconnect with the life force of the cosmos, and essentially, reclaim the missing parts of our Soul and the Soul of the world. I do not encourage turning from logic and reason, but rather to remember that we need more than these to live a soulful and healthy life.

Beyond reason, that logic-based realm of causal relationships and linear time, are many dimensions of what David Bohm called the implicate and super-implicate orders. He saw the universe as being made up of dimensions that we could not fully perceive or even theorize. Bohm understood the process of life to be an unfolding of the mysterious layers hidden within each observable layer. More and more, people are discovering that the world is not defined by only those things we can quantitatively prove or measure. Through intuitive practices such as these Rituals, we can delve into the subtle and mysterious planes long described by the mystics and shamans: subtle and mysterious places within you, through you, and beyond you.

However, I must emphasize that spiritual enlightenment is not something that you can simply procure through certain processes. Whether you gain insights or facilitate shifts depends on some combination of your intentions and the support of the mysterious. Therefore, approach these Rituals and all of your spiritual work with a spirit of invitation. Invite the mystical into your life. Be open to it, accept its unexpected forms, and never take it for granted. Showing up intuitively, opening your imaginal mind, is the first critical step to transforming your life with Ritual.

Though the pursuit of mystical understanding and connection still remains in the margins of our mainstream culture, we seekers and soul-tenders make up a large and interconnected global sub-culture. Some call us the Rainbow Tribe, a community of like-minded soul-tenders of every color, from many cultural heritages. Know that you are a member of this tribe, and as you explore yourself, you explore the cosmos. As you heal yourself, you heal the world.

May you walk in beauty. May your journey be blessed and bring forth blessings with each step you take.

Notes

Tending the Soul With Healing Ritual

Rituals List Appendix

Chapter 3: Earth — 49

  Sandpaintings: Mandala Rituals — 51

    Sandpainting 1: Clearing and Releasing — 53

    Sandpainting 2: Mythic Mirror — 56

    Extenstions & Adaptations — 59

  Darkspring Khuya Ritual: The Clearing Stone — 61

    Awakening Your Medicine Stone — 62

    Using Your Medicine Stone — 65

  Harmony Ritual: Attune With Nature — 67

Chapter 4: Water — 73

  Rainbow Shower — 76

    Adaptation: Salt & Soda Bath — 78

  Florida Water — 78

    Florida Water Recipe — 79

    Ritual Uses for Your Florida Water — 83

    Adaptation: Qi Drinking Water — 86

  Reflection Pool Ritual — 86

Chapter 5: Air — 91

  Sun & Moon Salutation — 92

    Adaptation: Drinking the Light — 95

  Walking Mantra Meditation — 96

    The Movement — 98

The Mantra	99
Adaptation: Walking a Labyrinth	107

Chapter 6: Fire 109

Fire Ceremony	110
Adaptation: Candle/Incense Variation	115
Fire Breaking Ice Ritual	116

Resources Appendix & Cited Sources

This Appendix lists the sources cited in the text, as well as a few resources with which you can further your explorations.

Bohm, David and Basil Hiley. *The Undivided Universe: An Ontological Interpretation of Quantum Theory.*

Braden, Greg. *The Spontaneous Healing of Belief: Shattering the Paradigm of False Limits.*

Chopra, Deepak. *Quantum Healing.*

Corbin, Henry. *Mundus Imaginalis.*

Delgado, Jorge Luis and MaryAnn Male. *Andean Awakening: An Inca Guide to Mystical Peru.*

Deloria, Vine, Jr. *C.G. Jung and the Sioux Traditions: Dreams, Visions, Nature and the Primitive.*

Drake, Michael. *The Shamanic Drum.*

---. Blog: *shamanicdrumming.com.*

Eden, Donna. *Energy Medicine.*

Eliade, Mircea. *The Sacred and the Profane.*

Emoto, Masaru. *Hidden Messages in Water.*

---. *The Healing Power of Water.*

Harner, Michael. *The Way of the Shaman.*

Ingerman, Sandra. *Speaking with Nature: Awakening to the Deep Wisdom of the Earth.*

Institute of HeartMath. "FAQ." heartmath.org. Judith, Anodea. *Wheels of Life.*

Jung, Carl Gustav. "Synchronicity: An Acausal Connecting Principle." *The Collected Works: Complete Digital Edition.*

Larsen, Stephen. *The Mythic Imagination.*

McGaa, Ed Eagleman. *Rainbow Tribe: Ordinary People Journeying on the Red Road.*

Powers, William K. *Yuwipi: Vision and Experience in Oglala Ritual.*

Reid, David. *Shambhala Guide to Chinese Medicine.*

Robbins, Anthony. Workshops & Resources: tonyrobbins.com.

Slattery, Dennis Patrick. *Riting Myth, Mythic Writing: Exploring Your Personal Myth.*

Smith, C. Michael. *Jung and Shamanism in Dialogue: Retrieving the Soul, Retrieving the Sacred.*

Smith, Huston. *Forgotten Truth: The Common Vision of the World's Religions.*

Smith, Jonathan Z. *Imagining Religion: From Babylon to Jonestown.*

Tarnas, Richard. *Cosmos and Psyche: Intimations of a New World View.*

Villoldo, Alberto. *Courageous Dreaming: How Shamans Dream the World into Being.*

Virtue, Doreen. *Healing with the Angels.*

Waters, Frank. *Book of the Hopi.*

Wilcox, Joan Parisi. *Masters of the Living Energy: The Mystical World of the Q'ero of Peru.*

Williams, J. E. *The Andean Codex: Adventures and Initiations Among the Peruvian Shamans.*

Wolff, Gay. Dissertation: *Applying Andean Shamanism to Healing Faustian Soul Loss: Re-Discovering the Subtle Realities of the Mundus Imaginalis.*

Wood, Nicholas Breeze, ed. *Sacred Hoop Magazine.* sacredhoop.org.

Tending the Soul With Healing Ritual

Index

A

Active Imagination 13, 14
Archetypes /Archetypal 6, 11-13, 15, 27-29, 34, 36, 39, 40, 43, 47, 52, 75, 84, 85, 92
Axis Mundi 8, 13, 21, 29, 30, 36
Ayni 7, 31, 33, 37, 38, 41, 47, 84, 85, 101, 112, 114

B

Bohm, David 14, 123, 129

C

Chakra 2, 23, 76, 77, 95, 96, 114

D

Depth psychology 11, 13, 39, 135

E

Emoto, Masaru 74, 81, 86, 89, 129

H

Heartmath 12, 130

I

Imagination 7, 8, 13-15, 25, 27, 43, 48, 63, 64, 109, 123

J

Jung, Carl 11, 13, 14, 36, 52, 129, 130

K

Kawsay (also see Living Energy) 8, 18, 19, 36, 50, 67, 75, 93

L

Light body (Luminous body) 8, 18, 19, 21, 22, 39, 73, 75, 77, 78, 96
    Rainbow body 18, 19
Living Energy
    Kawsay 8, 18, 19, 36, 50, 67, 75, 93
    Prana 8, 91, 93
    Qi 6, 8, 18, 21, 86, 91-93, 97

M

Mandala 42, 51-60
Mysticism 8, 14, 17, 18, 135
Myth 1, 10-13, 38, 86
Mythic 2, 5, 6, 10, 12, 13, 15-17, 21, 27, 29, 31-33, 35, 36, 38, 42, 43, 47, 48, 56, 58, 64, 75, 99, 102, 117, 118, 120, 135

P

Prana (also see Living Energy) 8, 91, 93

Q

Qi (also see Living Energy) 6, 8, 18, 21, 86, 91-93, 97
Quantum Physics 11, 15, 74, 86

S

Sacred Space 16, 35, 36, 38, 43, 44, 47, 53, 55, 56, 58, 60-62, 64, 67, 69, 70, 76-79, 81, 82, 84, 87, 89, 93, 96, 104, 112, 115, 116, 119, 120
Shamanism / Shamanic 8, 17, 28, 29, 18, 50, 79, 129, 130, 135
    Peruvian shamans, -ism 7, 18, 29, 84, 110, 131, 134, 135

U

Unconscious 6, 11, 13, 14, 20, 29, 30, 35, 36, 39, 40, 96, 97

Y

Yuwipi 16, 130

About the Author

For most of her adult life, Gay Wolff has been both a teacher and student. She has taught college English and literature classes for several decades, and has run retreats and led events for nearly as long. As a lifelong seeker of wisdom, she has been a student of body, mind, and soul, studying such fields as holistic health, energy medicine, psychology, hypnosis, mysticism, and shamanism. She holds a Ph.D. in Mythology with emphasis in Depth Psychology from Pacifica Graduate Institute, which bridges the academic and mythic interests of her life. Likewise, with this book, Gay strives to help bridge modern thinking with perennial wisdom: harmonizing the rational with the intuitive.

In addition to her academic studies, Gay has studied with Peruvian shamans for nearly a decade. Through her company, Sage Foundations, she provides Shamanic Energy Therapy and leads workshops and retreats to facilitate soul journey and soul tending experiences. She is available internationally for speaking engagements and workshops.

For more information, go to *sagefoundations.com*.

Tending the Soul With Healing Ritual

May your trails be crooked, winding, lonesome, dangerous, leading to the most amazing view.

~Edward Abbey

Made in the USA
San Bernardino, CA
27 November 2018